HEARTBEATS OF A TANKMAN
ECHOES OF COURAGE IN SILENCE

LT GEN A B SHIVANE

BLUEROSE PUBLISHERS
India | U.K.

Copyright © Lt Gen A B Shivane 2024

All rights reserved by author. No part of this publication may be reproduced, stored in a retrieval system or transmitted in any form or by any means, electronic, mechanical, photocopying, recording or otherwise, without the prior permission of the author. Although every precaution has been taken to verify the accuracy of the information contained herein, the publisher assumes no responsibility for any errors or omissions. No liability is assumed for damages that may result from the use of information contained within.

BlueRose Publishers takes no responsibility for any damages, losses, or liabilities that may arise from the use or misuse of the information, products, or services provided in this publication.

For permissions requests or inquiries regarding this publication, please contact:

BLUEROSE PUBLISHERS
www.BlueRoseONE.com
info@bluerosepublishers.com
+91 8882 898 898
+4407342408967

ISBN: 978-93-5989-721-9

Cover design: Muskan Sachdeva
Typesetting: Rohit

First Edition: March 2024

"Heartbeats of a Tankman"

Embark on an extraordinary poetic journey through the soul-stirring verses of "Heartbeats of a Tankman." Retired military officer Ashok Tankman, acclaimed for his bestselling works, unveils a new facet of his literary prowess in this collection. Poignantly written during the COVID-19 hiatus, these poems delve into diverse facets of life, offering a rare glimpse into the profound world of a soldier's experiences.

Structured with meticulous artistry, each poem is a heartfelt tribute to the sacrifices and valour of soldiers who have served India before and after independence. Themes such as family heritage, brave battles, love, destiny, and humanity weave together, capturing the essence of the author's military journey. The verses, accompanied by Hindi couplets and insightful abstracts, create a visually engaging experience.

"Heartbeats of a Tankman" transcends the ordinary, immersing readers in the soldier's perspective with profound insights and relatable emotions. Whether connected to the military or a poetry enthusiast, this collection promises a lasting impact, celebrating the indomitable human spirit and the transformative power of poetry. This book stands as a poignant homage, resonating with sacrifice, valour, love, and positivity—a literary masterpiece that delves into the very core of our souls.

THE SAGA OF THE PEN VERSUS THE SWORD

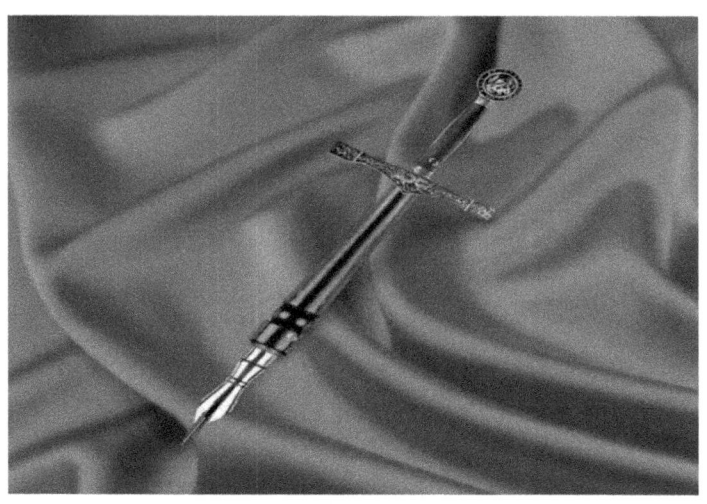

"Pens can't quell a dragon's flame,
Nor do swords craft poetic verse,
Mighty is the soul that wisely learns,
When to embrace the pen's tender grace,
When to yield the sword's fiery blaze."

…Ashok_Tankman

DEDICATION

(Pic Courtesy – ShemarooMe)

In the heat of the Kurukshetra battle, a remarkable conversation unfolded between the fearless Pandava warrior Arjuna and the divine Lord Krishna. In this hallowed dialogue, Lord Krishna shared profound spiritual insights, eventually transcribed into the revered Hindu scripture known as **'The Bhagavad Gita'**. Exploring the wisdom held within this sacred text is a privilege and a blessing. With deep respect, I dedicate this book to Lord Krishna and the Divine Shri Bhagavad Gita, recognising the timeless guidance it offers on our spiritual path.

The poem **'Eternal Wisdom: Bhagavad Gita's Timeless Message'** is my sacred reverence to 'The Bhagavad

Gita', a widely read theistic science. The teachings of the Gita transcend the boundaries of time and culture, encompassing essential concepts such as duty (*dharma*), self-realisation, and spiritual enlightenment, including divine knowledge, devotion, and action (*yogas*).

> *"कर्मण्येवाधिकारस्ते मा फलेषु कदाचन।*
> *मा कर्मफलहेतुर्भूर्मा ते सङ्गोऽस्त्वकर्मणि॥"*
>
> *(Bhagavad Gita Chapter 2, Verse 47)*

"You have the right to perform your prescribed duties, but you are not entitled to the fruits of your actions. Never consider yourself to be the cause of the results of your activities, and never be attached to not doing your duty."

Eternal Wisdom: Bhagavad Gita's Timeless Message

Kurukshetra, the land where heroes stood grand,
Arjuna faced a dilemma, a battle close at hand.
Krishna, the divine charioteer, spoke wisdom profound,
Guiding Arjuna's spirit; their truth now resounds.

With a bow in hand and a heart heavy with doubt,
"Can we fight kin?" Arjuna's inner voice did shout.
Krishna, Lord of all creation, voiced dharma's sacred call,
"To fulfil our noble duty, to stand firm and tall."

Divine knowledge, devotion, and action intertwined,
The path to self-realisation, where inner light will shine.
Release ego's binding chains, embrace the self in all,
Within the Gita's profound wisdom, hear your inner call.

Through every trial and tribulation, Gita's truth endures,
As life's journey unfolds, its wisdom remains pure.
Though battles may change, lessons stay the same,
In Bhagavad Gita's radiance, we find our divine aim.

Oh, the Bhagavad Gita, a timeless sacred text,
Teaching life lessons, where righteousness connects.
In the heart of our existence, where choices often meet,
The Gita's divine wisdom guides our wandering feet.

Heed the Gita's call, with courage and righteous might,
To live a life of purpose, bathed in harmony and light.
In every breath, let Lord Krishna be your guide,
In the Bhagavad Gita, our souls shall forever reside.

FOREWORD

Accomplished leaders in the armed forces are distinguished in many traits, but two stand out: Operational grasp and a sensitive nature. Lt Gen Ashok Shivane stands out on both counts.

He joined our Regiment, the war distinguished 7th Light Cavalry in 1978, and by dint of his professional excellence rose to 3 Star rank, commanding an Armoured Division, Strike1 and finally being at the helm of the mechanised forces.

We had the opportunity to work together in one of the largest exercises undertaken by the Indian Army- Yodha Shakti, where I was much impressed by his operational grasp and ability to orchestrate large scale manoeuvre like the Conductor of a symphony orchestra.

But more than his operational grasp, what distinguished him from his peers was his sensitivity to the human aspects, which is the core of any uniformed organisation. Coming from a lineage of proud soldiering over generations has only added to the lore.

This collection of poems and musings penned by the General, only reinforces this image. He reveals through his written and unsaid words, the heart of a distinguished and sensitive soldier.

It is my proud privilege to present this collection.

Lt. Gen. A.K. Singh

Erstwhile Army Commander & Lt Governor

ACKNOWLEDGEMENT

I am grateful to the gang of ***"Three Musketeers"*** *(my wife Sudha and my two daughters – Neha and Nidhi)* who have been my steadfast lifeline through all seasons, turning even the harshest of winters into spring's blossom. Their soulful bonding, like a well-oiled machine, has seamlessly extended to encompass my two wonderful sons-in-law and the apple of my eye, my charming granddaughter. Together, they form an exceptional team that has not only helped me navigate the storms of life but also celebrate every precious moment. I owe them my gratitude for inspiring me to embark on the journey of penning this book. Their patience and support have been my companions during the solitary hours spent in the world of poetic trance.

I humbly acknowledge the initiation vibes and constructive feedback from my younger son-in-law **Ritesh Sinha** who painstakingly read my script and gave publication advice, being an accomplished author. Also, my elder daughter **Neha** who gave me thematic ideas and collected pictures for my poems. I thank, Mrs. **Bela Sharma**, my Regimental lady, and a part of the extended family who infused the idea of a

Hindi verse or line in the structure to give it a unique character. My gratitude to **Dr Nidhi Umang Budhraja** for the encouragement and positivity to don this path and for infusing the light of spirituality in me. Her contribution to proof reading my script has been immense.

I am most grateful to my Regimental Officer **Lt Gen AK Singh, PVSM, AVSM, VSM, SM (Retd)** erstwhile Army Commander and Lieutenant Governor of Andaman and Nicobar Islands, and Puducherry for penning the *'Foreword'*. He has been the most professionally respected military leader, administrator par excellence and above all a great human being. Having served under him, I have been a witness to them all. Indeed, a Cavalier and a Man of Steel. I have been fortunate to have him in my life as a friend, philosopher, and guide.

Lastly, I salute the **Indian Army and the Armoured Corps** who gave me the eternal soul of a soldier. This journey called *'Life'* would never have been complete without them. Wearing the uniform and ***being a Tankman is God's blessing*** and a privilege of the chosen few, which I cherish every moment of my life and wish for at every birth.

INTRODUCTION

I have never been a poet, nor had the time or inclination for poetry when in uniform. Post-retirement employment opportunities followed with a short break due to COVID-19. It was during this hiatus that I penned a few poems and became a so-called poet by default. I gave my pen name as *'Ashok_ Tankman'*. However, my true realisation came after April 2023 when my latest book, *'Professional Military Education – Making of the 21st Century Warrior,'* was published and achieved recognition as one of the new bestsellers in its category. This recognition made me aware of my penchant for writing books, in addition to the over 130 periodicals, papers, and articles I had written post-retirement. I now ventured into the unknown world of poetry.

The inspiration to delve into the world of writing and embark on this venture, a book of poems, came from my wife **Sudha**, my elder daughter **Neha** and my younger son-in-law, **Ritesh.** It was entirely a greenfield endeavour for me. What followed were poems that touched upon various facets of life, culminating in the creation of this book titled **'Heartbeats of a Tankman.'** The choice of the title was intuitive and straight from the heart.

In contrast to my previous books or periodicals which required research, poems demanded an entirely different mindset—moods. While retirement gave me time, the mood swings were diverse – from emotional nationalism to youthful romanticism, as reflected in the diverse poems within the book. Crafting poetry also demanded solitude, allowing me to lose myself in the realm of emotions, nostalgic memories, and timelessness reminiscence. This process usually occurred during the peaceful hours of the morning, late at night, or on occasions when emotions touched a chord.

These poems embody the lifetime blessings of God Almighty and the gratitude of all those who enriched my journey called life. In the words of the renowned Hindi poet Harivansh Rai Bachchan, my journey can be best described.

"निकले थे अकेले मंज़िल की ओर,
लोग मिलते गए और कारवाँ बनता गया।"

ABSTRACT

'Heartbeats of a Tankman' is an extraordinary bouquet of poems that delve into the profound and multifaceted world of a soldier's experiences. Through the lens of the author's journey in uniform, these verses take readers on a poignant exploration of themes that resonate deeply with the human spirit.

The poems in this collection offer a unique perspective, weaving together the threads of the author's military life, his family's heritage, and the stories of soldiers who have served their nation both before and after independence. Each poem is a heartfelt tribute to the sacrifices and valour of those who have worn the uniform or participated in India's freedom struggle, providing readers with a window into the soul of a soldier.

As readers traverse the pages of this collection, they will encounter themes that range from *'Saga of Family Heritage, Bravehearts and Battles, Tryst with Love and Destiny to Humans for Humanity'*. These themes reflect the life, soul, heart and emotions of the author. Each poem carries a powerful message, inviting contemplation on the human condition, the bonds of camaraderie among soldiers, and the enduring spirit of resilience.

Structured in a visually engaging layout, *'Heartbeats of a Tankman'* pairs each poem with a brief relationship to the author's experiences or emotions, an abstract that offers a glimpse into the poem's essence, and a Hindi couplet that beautifully encapsulates its sentiments. This unique format not only enhances the reading experience but also allows readers to connect more deeply with the emotions conveyed in each verse.

What sets *'Heartbeats of a Tankman'* apart is its ability to convey the soldier's perspective through the artistry of verse. It immerses readers in the world of soldiering, evoking emotions and insights that are at once profound and relatable. Whether you have a personal connection to the military or simply appreciate the beauty of poetry, this collection promises to leave a lasting impact on your heart and mind.

'Heartbeats of a Tankman', stands as a heartfelt homage to the soldier's journey. It celebrates the indomitable human spirit and serves as a testament to the profound impact of poetry, delving into the very core of our souls. This literary work is sure to strike a chord with readers, providing a window into a realm characterised by sacrifice, valour, love and positivity.

ये एक टैंकमन के दिल के परवाने हैं,
जीवन के हर धड़कन के अफसाने हैं।

CONTENTS

THE SAGA OF THE PEN VERSUS THE SWORD iv
DEDICATION v
FOREWORD viii
ACKNOWLEDGEMENT x
INTRODUCTION xii
ABSTRACT xiv

SAGA OF FAMILY HERITAGE

MY LIFE'S JOURNEY CALLED FAUJ 1
ECHOES OF RUINS ONCE HOME 11
ODE TO MY SOLDIER, MY FATHER, MY BEST FRIEND 14
AN ANGEL CALLED MITRA – MY LOVING MOM 17
MY SOLDIER.. MY BRAVEHEART.. MY BROTHER 20
SISTER: MY GUIDING LIGHT 23
THE LOVE OF MY LIFE 26
MY DAUGHTERS, MY TREASURES 29
ODE TO MY BELOVED CANINE FRIENDS 31
I AM A TANKMAN, A MAN OF STEEL 34

BRAVEHEARTS AND BATTLES

CHHATRAPATI SHIVAJI MAHARAJ: THE RADIANT LEGACY 39
ECHOES OF SARAGARHI: A TRIBUTE TO COURAGE 42
VALOUR AT HAIFA: THE CAVALRY CHARGE 45
WAILS OF JALLIANWALA WALLS 48
ODE TO THE AZAD HIND FAUJ 51
BRAVE HEARTS OF INDIA'S FREEDOM STRUGGLE 54
ODE TO GALLANT HORSEMEN AND TANKMEN 57
CELEBRATING INDIA'S FREEDOM SYMPHONY 60

ZOJILA 1948 – THE SAVIOUR OF LADAKH	63
GUARDIANS OF THE TRICOLOUR	66
THE LOVE OF UNIFORM	69
A TRIBUTE TO MY TANKMEN MENTORS	72
THE CRADLE OF MILITARY LEADERSHIP	75
WE ARE GOLFIES, CAN'T YOU SEE	78
WORLD OF ARMY ANECDOTES	81
KARGIL: THE HOME OF IMMORTAL BRAVES	88
BRAVEHEARTS OF GALWAN	91
BALIDAAN : ODE TO THE BRAVE HEARTS OF RAJOURI	94
BRUTAL TRUTH OF WAR	97
THE FALLEN SOLDIER	100
THE ECHOES OF ELUSIVE PEACE	103

TRYST WITH LOVE AND DESTINY

ECHOES OF A VANISHING EDEN	107
CHEERS TO OUR GIRLFRIENDS AND WIVES.... MAY THEY NEVER MEET	110
AGE IS JUST A FUNNY NUMBER	113
CELEBRATING LORD KRISHNA'S DIVINE BIRTH	116
LOVE BEYOND DESTINY	119
BOUNDLESS LOVE: A SYMPHONY OF SOULFUL HEARTS	121
MAKING MEMORIES, NOT DREAMS	124
ODE TO THE NOBLE STEEDS	127
ENCHANTING HAZEL EYES	130
SOMEONE.... SOMEWHERE.... SOMEDAY	133
EMBERS OF CANDLELIGHT	136
THOSE WERE THE DAYS MY FRIEND	139
THE RAY OF HOPE	142
WHEN COMPASSION ECHOES	145
EMBRACE THE JOY OF SMILE	148

HUMANS FOR HUMANITY

GOLF: A LIFE'S ECSTASY	151
HUMANS FOR HUMANITY	154

JOURNEY OF CONNECTION: THE BRIDGE OF LIFE	157
SENTINELS OF MOTHER EARTH	160
SPIRITUAL JOURNEY: AWAKENING OF THE SOUL	163
SWAY IN THE RHYTHM OF LIFE	166
SWEET SURRENDER	169
MYSTIC FLOWERS: GARDEN OF LIFE	172
LIFE'S SPLENDOUR: A SYMPHONY OF HEARTS	175
WHISPERS OF SILENCE	178
AWAKENING OF LIFE'S ESSENCE	181
EPILOGUE	184

MY LIFE'S JOURNEY CALLED FAUJ

(Pic: Author at NDA, as a Lt Gen and then a Veteran)

Well, who am I? I am just a soldier who had the good fortune to walk astride many great soldiers in my journey called Fauj. I was born a Fauji and will breathe my last as a Fauji. My body has been blessed to have donned the prestigious uniform; my mind moulded to the selfless ideals of a soldier, my emotions painted in shades of Olive Green, my dreams entwined with the tricolour, and my soul forever bound to the life of a soldier.

The stars on my shoulder and the medals adorning my chest are my most precious eternal treasures. I most humbly owe it to the men I had the honour to command and the guidance cum mentorship of many seniors whom I served under during my varied tenures. Though I no longer don the uniform, it remains an indelible part of my eternal soul, and so I proudly call myself a "Soldier4Life."

Retirement has merely re-attired me, allowing me to continue my enduring mission of "Aspire to Inspire" before I transit from being "Distinguished to Extinguished." I firmly believe that our country's flag doesn't flutter solely because of the winds, but because of the last breaths of our soldiers who've sacrificed their lives to protect it. So 'Veer Naris/Veer Families' is a very emotive issue close to my heart.

My journey began as a Fauji brat in a military hospital in Ambala, the third sibling in my family. Interestingly, that very hospital was later bombed during a war and then rebuilt. My father hailed from a traditional Maharashtrian background, while my mother came from an affluent Punjabi family in pre-partition Lahore. Their love story, a tale of meeting at a defence club, dancing romantically, and culminating in a love marriage, initially shook both their families due to inter-caste barriers. Yet soon my mom's loving nature endured her to all. She became from Mitra to 'Mitraakka' ('akka' – elder sister).

My upbringing was a joyous experience within a wonderful family, including our beloved dogs, Timmy and Paro. Our family was characterised by its values, secular outlook, discipline, and deeply ingrained ethics.

My father, a man of both compassion and unwavering discipline, hailed from the small town of Osmanabad, Maharashtra. In a rare feat of his time, he earned his engineering degree from Osmania University in Urdu. He was a staunch nationalist, even enduring imprisonment as a student freedom fighter during India's freedom struggle. In 1943, he joined the Royal Air Force, initially flying 'Spitfires' before being transferred to the Royal Sappers in 1945, when they discovered his engineering expertise. He earned the nickname 'Shivyane' due to the challenge of pronouncing Indian names. Shivyane, a young officer, was stationed at General (later Field Marshal) William Slim's headquarters in Burma during World War II. In those days the British Army had a field mobile cinema unit to screen war movies and newsreels for the troops. One day, Shivyane and his Indian friend drove in a Willys Jeep to the screening location. However, they were stopped at the entrance by a British Military Police personnel who declared that Indians weren't allowed to bring their Jeep inside. Young Shivyane, in a fit of anger, slapped him and sped away refusing to see the movie. The next day, he was brought before Gen Slim in his

Sam Browne (official dress) for disciplinary action. Gen Slim bellowed, 'March him in!' The charges of manhandling were read, and Gen Slim, in a stern voice, said, 'Shivyane, you've committed a crime. I'll spare you this time due to your exemplary service record, but if I were you, I'd do it again and again.' Then he ordered, 'March him out.' Such were the leadership qualities of those stalwart men of steel from that era. My father retired as a Lieutenant Colonel with the AVSM award, having earned immense respect and accolades during his distinguished career. In his own words, "An officer may eventually hang up his uniform, but hanging up his spurs after a distinguished and unblemished career is a joy that grows eternally."

My mother, an accomplished educationist, was an adored student of Madam Montessori herself. She was the pillar of strength of our family, gracefully managing the long absences of my father due to his military duties. She made many silent sacrifices for the smiles of the family. She was a strong, calm, and elegant lady, the embodiment of selfless love. Her heart for the well-being of soldier families and her love for the army knew no bounds.

My brother followed in my father's footsteps, joining the military and eventually becoming a subaltern in the Infantry (Gurkha Rifles) in November 1971, on the eve of the war. My sister, my confidante, and my secret keeper married the Olive Green, adding lustre to our family history.

Life was like an ECG, with its ups and downs balanced by equal measures of happiness and sorrow. The most unforgettable tragedy struck on March 5, 1972, when my brother, a young subaltern with only three months of service, lost his life at the Chinese border due to a freak lightning strike. He had worn a uniform since the age of 10 as a Rimcollian, cherishing it for a mere three months post-commissioning before making the ultimate sacrifice for our nation. Today, his name, 2Lt D B Shivane, is engraved on the walls of the National War Memorial. He remains my icon of a soldier and a gentleman. The impact on our family was profound, but with time, as many soldier's families do, we found a way to reconcile with our destiny and move on.

Behind the scenes, I was a positive and fun-loving youngster, yet in the spotlight, I was a shy individual. Life, for me, was a romantic journey, guided by principles of love, care, and grace. The concept of "On parade and Off parade" was instilled in me during my formative years. Being the youngest and pampered, I often got away with my wishes. I received the best of a convent education and enjoyed a great quality of life. I was considered a bright student, though not always the top-ranking type. Outdoor sports, picnics, Fauji parties, and club gatherings were integral to my life.

As someone who let the heart lead the head, I remained a fun-loving positive guy. My youthful infatuations kept my heart forever young and from a teenager, I grew into a 'senager' (senior citizen + teenager). My enduring passion for dance and music added splendour to my life. Yet, the profound impressions of military life etched themselves deeper with each passing day. I witnessed the 1962, 1965, and 1971 wars from the perspective of a budding soldier, often accompanying my mother to the Military Hospital to visit the wounded warriors. The sight of tanks at crossroads and the entrances of military establishments always sent my adrenaline soaring. It was during those days that I metaphorically cloaked myself in the identity of a "Tankman". The military became my most cherished dream, my way of life, and the tank, my love, my passion, and my ultimate destination.

After completing school, where my subjects were geared toward a medical career, I cleared the MBBS entrance exam following some coaching classes. However, my heart was set on the NDA exam, my lifeline. I will never forget my father's unwavering support for my decision to forego MBBS and join the NDA, despite the lingering pain of losing my young brother in harness, which haunted my parents until their last days.

And so, I embarked on my military journey, passing out from the IMA and being commissioned into the illustrious and oldest Regiment of the Armoured Corps, the "7th Light Cavalry," proudly bearing the motto "We Lead." I became the first cavalry officer in my family.

As life unfolded, I married a soulful and lovely girl, a second-generation Fauji brat. My father-in-law was a gentleman and a saintly soldier, while his father had proudly served as the Military Secretary to the Maharaja of Rewa. Their proud soldier heritage was evident in their way of life. We were blessed with two daughters, and now, a granddaughter who has become the apple of our eyes.

My family's military legacy extended across all three branches of the armed forces. My aunt married an RAF/IAF officer, and my niece married a promising naval aviator. Within the army, we had representatives in nearly all arms and services, with me being the lone Tankman.

Our family exemplified love and happiness, embodying the spirit of national integration. My Punjabi mother married my Maharashtrian father in 1949. My sister was wedded to a Punjabi Signal's Army officer of repute and me to a Punjabi girl. My elder daughter married a

Kashmiri Sikh, and my younger one wed a Bihari gentleman, further enriching our secular outlook on life.

My life, both in and out of uniform, revolved around the timeless wisdom of Field Marshal Philip Chetwode, expressed during the inauguration of IMA on December 10, 1931: *"The safety, honour, and welfare of your country come first, always and every time; The honour, welfare, and comfort of the men you command come next; Your own ease, comfort, and safety come last, always and every time."*

Subconsciously, I added the adjective "happiness" to this creed, making the well-being of my command an even more integral part of my leadership philosophy as I rose in rank and age. I firmly believe that a good leader leads by example from the front, but a great leader also creates many leaders through their influence within the team. It's always "WE" and not "I," emphasising the importance of unwavering integrity. My happiness stemmed from sharing and caring for my command, and their success was the greatest reward for maintaining the highest standards of training for war.

My journey progressed from a 2nd Lieutenant Troop Leader of Tanks in 1978, serving in the illustrious and one of the oldest Cavalry Regiments, the "7th Light Cavalry," to raising a new Armoured Regiment, "50 Armoured Regiment," and eventually having the privilege of commanding it. Along the way, I held numerous ranks and appointments, culminating in my appointment as a Strike Corps Commander and then as the Director General Mechanised Forces. I finally hung my spurs on 31st December 2017.

My life in uniform spanned nearly four decades, a heavenly blessing bestowed by the God Almighty. Retirement brought new challenges to my body, mind, and soul, but I remained steadfast in my commitment to uphold the respect of the uniform and the dignity of rank. Fortunately, I was offered a meaningful role by the Ministry of Defence, serving as a Consultant for the Ordnance Factory Board until July 2020.

The fateful year 2020, marred by the COVID-19 pandemic, became a year of learning, rejuvenation, and opportunities. I began to explore and unveil my bucket list, delving into writing, poetry, music, and spirituality. I kept myself physically and mentally active, firmly believing that age is merely a number. My newfound talent for analytical writing and motivational talks emerged. I authored two books and contributed to two more, with one of them becoming an international new category bestseller in 2023. I also dedicated my energy to motivating young people to become COVID warriors, arming themselves against the virus with body, mind, and soul. I played an active role as a

"COVID WARRIOR," earning accolades and awards for my efforts. Additionally, I invested my energy in environmental protection and social causes. My love for golf, cycling and travelling, being close to nature, flourished even more.

Yet, at the core, I remain a 'Soldier4Life' with my first love always being "THE TANK". My pen name for my poems reflects this passion: 'Ashok_Tankman'.

> *"ऐ वतन, ऐ वतन, हमको तेरी क़सम,*
> *तेरी राहों में जाँ तक लुटा जायेंगे,*
> *फूल क्या चीज़ है तेरे क़दमों पे हम,*
> *भेंट अपने सरों की चढ़ा जायेंगे।"*

ECHOES OF RUINS ONCE HOME

(Pic -House Of Pandit Shiv Narayan Agnihotri, Edward Road, Lahore, Pakistan)

Pandit Shiv Narayan Agnihotri (1850-1929), the esteemed founder of Dev Samaj, holds a cherished place in my family lineage as my maternal great grandfather. His life was an unwavering dedication to both religious enlightenment and social welfare. Nestled within the walls of a magnificent Haveli in Lahore, the family thrived as a close-knit, joyous joint unit. My mother, the youngest among her siblings, regaled us with stories of the haveli's warmth, bonding, and even moments of shared sorrow.

The tumultuous era of Partition ushered in a torrent of tribulations and separations. Tragedy struck when my uncle, Balabh Agnihotri, fell victim to a college murder.

Those nights were fraught with anxiety as they patrolled the rooftop, armed with chilli flakes, clutching a knife, a last-resort measure for preserving dignity. Eventually, the family migrated to Delhi. The haveli still stands as a monument in ruins.

'Echoes of Ruins Once Home', stands as a poignant and introspective poem. It explores the fleeting nature of life and possessions, chronicling the poignant transformation of a once-vibrant joint family home into a solemn relic. Amidst this transformation, it eloquently captures the enduring allure of nature's resilience and the enduring memories of the garden and its lively inhabitants.

एक हवेली की दीवारों की यह कहानी,
आज भी बीती यादों की दीवानी।

Echoes of Ruins Once Home

In a house that once resounded with laughter and cheer,
Now stands in silence, reminiscing about yesteryears.
A joint family's abode, where love would appear,
Celebrating many a season, through joy and tears.

Peacocks waltzed, a daily vibrant display,
Bulbuls, sparrows, parrots, in their sweet way.
A rainbow of blossoms in the sun's warm rays,
In memories, their presence forever to stay.

The garden, once nurtured by a gentle hand,
With Gul Mohar and Ashoka, a verdant land.
Yet, nature reclaims its space, recasts the sand,
Vibrant hues vanished, and ruins in solitude stand.

Once bursting with life, now an empty shell,
A repository of tales where memories dwell.
Homes cherished, yet a truth we must tell,
In the end, possessions fade, but stories swell.

Homes expand, as families dwindle and shrink,
Seeking solitude, when the house is at its brink.
Yet when the nest is vacant, we start to rethink,
Cherished family lost, as we stand on fate's brink.

In destiny's grand scheme, they find cause to jest,
Humans who build, finally leave their own nest.
Journey of life, truth of destination the ultimate test,
Seeking pastures, we leave putting everything to rest.

ODE TO MY SOLDIER, MY FATHER, MY BEST FRIEND

My father, Lt. Col. B. V. Shivane, AVSM (Retd), was a remarkable soldier of the WW2 era. He was not only a freedom fighter in college but also a distinguished war veteran both pre and post-independence. His achievements included accolades from Former PM Pandit Jawaharlal Nehru for his contributions to Op Amar Project, and he was later awarded the AVSM by the President of India for his distinguished service. As Commander of the 13 BRTF, he earned the admiration of the King of Bhutan and its people for his extraordinary efforts in building roads under hazardous conditions. In the 1962 War, during a special mission, he was declared 'Missing - dead or alive not known' for over three months, only to resurface victorious after completing his mission, surviving on jungle fruits and roots. This cost him his health in the long term, but he never attributed it to it.

I had not known a hero till I saw my father in uniform. Beyond his military prowess, he had a romantic heart and a positive outlook on life. His smart demeanour, unwavering discipline, and integrity shaped him into a multifaceted and deeply cherished individual whom I always held in the highest esteem. Frequently, our communication transcended beyond mere words, through simple hand-holding or exchanged glances, for our unspoken connection was profound. Even today, he continues to be my guiding light from the celestial realm above.

पिता ने देश के लिए वर्दी पहनकर दिखाया हमें,
हर मुश्किल में आगे बढ़ना, यह सबक सिखाया हमें।

Ode to My Soldier, My Father, My Best Friend

In the realm of memories, where legends reside,
There's a figure revered, my father, my pride.
A friend, a philosopher, my idol, my knight,
Whose valorous tales illuminate the darkest night.

A World War II veteran, his bravery left an indelible mark,
A soldier who ignited victory, kindling hope with his spark.
Through countless battles, he stood resolute and strong,
For the honour of his nation, he persevered all along.

An engineer by profession, a mastermind of creation,
He crafted bridges and roads beyond imagination.
But within his uniform, a gentle soul did reside,
Whose kindness and compassion could never hide.

Through life's turbulent journey, he forged the way,
With family at his core, love's eternal sway.
He blessed all he met, with a soul so rare,
Leaving imprints of kindness, everywhere.

Oh, I miss you my soldier, my father, my dearest friend,
Your guidance and wisdom, on which I ever depend.
Though your mortal form has found its rightful rest,
Your immortal soul guides me, on life's test.

In the bliss of heaven, may peace be on your side,
Surrounded by joy, with my loving mom beside.
May your noble soul forever watch over our days,
Infusing us with strength, love's everlasting rays.

AN ANGEL CALLED MITRA – MY LOVING MOM

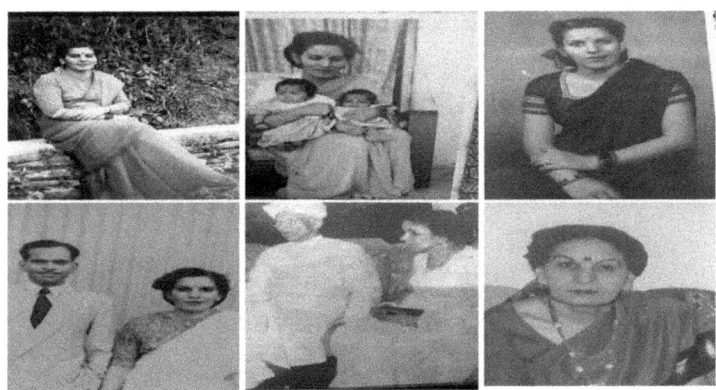

Mitra is a sanskrit word which means friend. My mother, Mitra Shivane (maiden name Mitra Agnihotri) was an extraordinary and graceful woman of her time. She was a woman of substance and a mother whose sacrifice for the family's happiness knew no bounds. A strong exterior with a soft heart, she braved many turbulences of life… from her husband being declared 'missing dead or alive not known' in the 1962 War, the tragic death of a 20-year-old son, and combating cancer with a smile. Yet she never let her frozen tears ever drop in front of her children. Her love for grandchildren remained supreme. An iconic woman of empowerment and style, she visited the hair stylist regularly until her last days. Her wardrobe would be the envy of every woman even today. I remained her spoiled brat who could do no wrong. Her blessings are always with the family.

'An Angel Called Mitra – My Loving Mom', is an ode to my mom Mitra, whose life is depicted as a testament to grace, love, and resilience. Even in their physical absence, Mother's love and spirit continue to shine as a guiding force, leaving behind an inspiring and radiant legacy for her loved ones to cherish and uphold.

मित्रा परिवार का एक अनमोल हीरा थी,
यादों का कारवाँ, दिलों की धड़कन थी,
आज भी वो हमें देती है आसमान से आशीर्वाद,
हर पल उनके लम्हों की दास्तान आती है याद।

An Angel Called Mitra – My Loving Mom

An Angel called Mitra, a woman of grace,
Her starry eyes glow, from celestial space.
A lady of substance, an eternal mother divine,
Boundless love and memories forever to enshrine.

Lahore's Dev Samaj family, a respected name with fame,
Partition made her a refugee, but she rose like a flame.
Educationist par excellence with inspiring teaching flair,
Igniting young minds, knowledge and wisdom to share.

1949 love story, a dashing young captain stole her heart,
In the Central Vista Mess, they waltzed love to start.
Inter-caste woes, their dark shadows did cast,
Love triumphed, and she soon won all hearts.

Soon she became the daughter of both homes,
Compassion and love for her ever roamed.
Young to old, she was the idol of every soul,
Lighting their lives with joy was her noble role.

An Army wife, she brought smiles to war wounded,
Comforted widows and orphans love unbounded.
Guiding soldier's families with touching care,
She became the happy place for many in despair.

Hey, Mom, miss you dearly; your love never truly fades,
Your spirit lingers, a part of you in our hearts cascades.
Your legacy endures, a radiant and guiding light,
Leading us through life, even in the darkest of nights.

MY SOLDIER.. MY BRAVEHEART..
MY BROTHER

Some dark memories are here to stay as a neverending bad dream. 5 March 1972, was a Sunday and it was to be a fun day. The family was awaiting with excitement to welcome home 2Lt D B Shivane, returning from his first leave next week. That peaceful evening at around 8 pm when dinner was to be served, the phone rang and the operator said a call from Nathula. The family, in excitement, gathered around to have a word with Dilip, the first being Dad who picked up the phone. But suddenly we saw Dad going pale and the only words he said thrice were "Yes... Yes" and "Yes" before putting the receiver down. Perplexed, we awaited his announcement which came as a storm – *'Baba (pet name of Dilip) is no more'*. He was killed by a freak lightning strike in the line of duty at the border post of Nathula on the India–China border in Sikkim. Dilip had graduated from RIMC, NDA and IMA with distinction and had a promising career ahead which destiny brought crashing down. Utter disbelief and trauma followed which remain beyond words. Just that he was a grand soldier, a Braveheart and my proud brother. "**Soldiers Never Die, They Ever Remain Young and Immortal.**"

The poem **'My Soldier.. My Braveheart.. My Brother'**, is a saga of the sacrifice and bravery of a soldier. In the context of a pivotal night in 1972, the poem conveys the intense emotions of anticipation, grief, and deep sorrow that enveloped the family upon learning of their son's demise while serving in the military. The verses vividly depict the soldier's steadfast dedication to duty, even in his youth, and the enduring influence of his presence on those who remained behind.

जो देश के लिए शहीद हुए उनको मेरा सलाम,
खून से जिस ज़मी को सींचा, उस ज़मीन को सलाम।

My Soldier.. My Braveheart.. My Brother

It was the fateful night of '72's embrace,
Awaiting your call with an excited face.
The phone's ring echoed, colours paled,
Message from beyond, sorrow unveiled.

Destined a brave soldier, a mission profound,
You stood unyielding; courage unbound.
Not yet 21, life's thread abruptly shorn,
Incomplete journey, leaving us to mourn.

Nathula's border, you stood upright,
Country's guardian, day and night.
In an instant, fate's hand rearranged,
A lightning strike, life's course estranged.

Laughter's resonance, memory's embrace,
Love and smiles, time can't erase.
Though departed, you linger so near,
In our hearts, your presence so dear.

In hearts, you live, in memories strong,
The light you brought, forever long.
Bravery and valour, a spirit ablaze,
Enduring strength, amidst life's maze.

Though you've departed, that fateful year,
You passed the baton, for us to steer.
Rest in peace brother, high above the blue,
As we carry your legacy so pure and true.

SISTER: MY GUIDING LIGHT

My parents had twins two years after marriage: my brother and sister. I came along six years later, the default child. My sister became my friend, philosopher, and guide, and often the watchful eye when I strayed. Her love and care had no bounds. Many a time she even confiscated gifts I bought for my girlfriends from my meagre pocket money. Of course, she did proudly announce that it was bought for her by a loving brother!! She later married an Army Signal officer of repute, had two kids and four grandkids, and excelled as a historian and academician. Her Shakespearian writings could put many writers to shame. I grew up in her shadow and now live nearby, so distance doesn't keep us apart. She remains my special happy place and a beacon of light.

'Sister: My Guiding Light', is a heartfelt exploration of the profound bond between siblings. This poem takes us on a journey through the shared memories of childhood, illustrating how the sister has been a constant presence through life's ups and downs. The poem celebrates the enduring love and connection between siblings, offering a touching tribute to the sister in the brother's life.

मेरी बहन, मेरी जिंदगी का सहारा,
हर मुश्किल और ख़ुशी में मेरा तारा।

Sister: My Guiding Light

In childhood's embrace, we used to play,
Through every season, come what may.
In her smile, I find my guiding star,
My loving sister, no matter how far.

She taught me to walk, to laugh, to dream,
In her wisdom, I found life's gleam.
Elder, wiser, a steadfast light,
Friend, philosopher, day and night.

Through life's twists and turns, we've swayed,
Her wisdom, like a beacon, never strayed.
In her counsel, I navigate my way,
Darkest nights and brightest days.

She's a friend who knows my every thought,
With her, my every secret safely caught.
She grabbed gifts for my girlfriend, so sweet,
Took them with a thank you, so complete,

Through thick and thin, she's always there,
With a heart so loving, so rare.
In her embrace, I find my peace,
My sister's love will never cease.

So here's to you, my sister, so dear,
With each passing day, each passing year.
Friend, philosopher, guide, and more,
In my life, you remain my inner core.

THE LOVE OF MY LIFE

They say marriages are made in heaven; a belief solidified by witnessing my parents' inter-caste love story. While their love story bloomed naturally, ours was an arranged marriage, but it was marked by an instant connection of souls and acceptance at first sight. Sudha Shorey transformed into Reetu Shivane, and I, a carefree bachelor, became a hubby dear. Together, we embarked on a journey that took us through numerous stations, both in life and love. She shouldered the immense responsibility of raising our children single-handedly during my long absences due to professional training or field assignments. A woman of unwavering faith, her prayers remained a source of strength and stability in our lives. As an Army wife, she not only cared for our family but also extended her support to the larger Army community. To me, she has always been my pillar of strength and enchanting inspiration during life's storms or moments of celebration.

This poem *'The Love of My Life'*, expresses the depth of love and bonding between the couple within the backdrop of the Army, which serves as not just a profession but a way of life.

ज़िंदगी के सफर में हर पल दिया है साथ,
बिन तुम्हारे, ये मंज़िल कभी न लगती खास।

The Love of My Life

With every smile that graces your face,
My world created our happy space.
We danced the salsa many a night,
Swaying to the music, romantic lights.

Seasons of joy and tempestuous weather,
We've grown in love, stronger together.
Wisdom and warmth, a steady guide,
In this journey of life, always by my side.

Together, we embarked on a journey profound,
Numerous stations, in life and love, we're bound.
You shouldered the responsibility with grace,
Raising our children in my absence's embrace.

Woman of unwavering faith, you've been my guide,
In your prayers, our strength and stability coincide.
As an Army wife, your support knew no bounds,
For our family and the Army, your love resounds.

Trials and triumphs, we've faced hand in hand,
Life's every challenge we shall ever withstand.
In your love, my life finds endless delight,
With you, my dear, everything feels just right.

So here's to you, my partner and wife,
Beloved, you are my heart's endless life.
With you, my love forever shall bloom,
Together, we'll conquer any shade of gloom.

MY DAUGHTERS, MY TREASURES

I have been blessed by two daughters and a granddaughter, who remain the most beautiful part of my world. Neha the elder was born by default exactly ten months after marriage and Nidhi the younger by design three years later. Seeing my daughters grow and blossom from toddlers to happily wedded professionals has been both a joy and a blessing of God Almighty. Yet the centre of focus and jewel of the family has been my darling granddaughter Anaisha who calls me Ashok_Tankman and stands motivated to join NDA in 2035.

The poem, titled **'My Daughters, My Treasures',** celebrates the profound and unconditional love between a father and his daughters. The poem portrays daughters as precious gems, filling one's life with genuine love and joy.

बेटियाँ हैं हर घर की रौशनी, भगवान का फरिश्ता,
उनके साथ जीवन सुनहरा, एक अनमोल रिश्ता।

My Daughters, My Treasures

In the cradle of my heart, a treasure I hold,
Daughters, my gem, more precious than gold.
With eyes that sparkle like the morning dew,
They fill my life with a love that's so true.

Their laughter, like a melody, fills the air,
A symphony of joy, a love so fair.
They dance through life with grace and might,
My daughters, my beacon in the darkest night.

I watched them grow from a tiny child,
With dreams in their heart, so wild.
I held their hands as they took their first stride,
Each passing day, my heart swelled with pride.

In my arms, a precious jewel, so rare,
My daughter's my love beyond compare.
Eyes that twinkle like the morning's grace,
In their embrace, I find my sacred space.

So let the world bear witness, let them see,
Love between a father and daughter, so free.
An unbreakable bond, a love so pure,
In their presence, my heart will forever endure.

One day they ventured to new homes far away,
Yet in my heart, their love forever stays.
As they embrace new life with partners so dear,
Our bond remains ever stronger over the years.

ODE TO MY BELOVED CANINE FRIENDS

Life without my beloved canine companions is simply inconceivable. I was fortunate to grow up alongside Timmy, a wise Lashai Terrier, who my senior, played the role of the boss when we were alone. Paro was a royal-blood Bhutanese Terrier and behaved as one. Timmy and Paro, were my closest childhood friends, imparting invaluable lessons of love, care, compassion, and unwavering loyalty. After I got married, Tuffy, a miniature Pomeranian, joined our family. He was a brave little warrior who often returned home from wild adventures with battle scars, yet his presence always warmed our hearts. The final additions to our furry family were Bonzo, a dignified black Labrador, and Cindy, an endearing white Labrador. Their boundless love and loyalty knew no limits and left an indelible mark on my wife and daughters as they grew into a bonded family. Though these beloved companions have now become twinkling stars in the starry sky, their memories will forever remain in our hearts.

'Ode To My Beloved Canine Friends', pays a heartfelt tribute to these loyal companions. This poem celebrates the enduring bond between humans and their dogs, capturing their unwavering loyalty, playfulness, and the lasting impact they leave. Even in their absence, the memories of these cherished friends continue to shine brightly, leaving paw prints on our souls.

तुमको मिलकर, जीवन सुनहरा बना,
तुम्हारी यादों का बेमिसाल कारवां बना।

Ode to My Beloved Canine Friends

Oh, loyal companions of fur and tail,
With eyes that gleam and hearts that sail.
Nostalgic memories of your love and joy,
Deep in my heart, I shall forever enjoy.

Your paws, like whispers in the night,
Guide me through the darkness with pure delight.
With each bound and playful bark,
You chased away shadows, even in the dark.

From sunrise's golden hues to twilight's grace,
You fill my life with love's warm embrace.
Through every season, unwavering and true,
My faithful friends, forever, I cherish you.

In gardens, you danced with boundless glee,
Souls so pure, wild, untamed, forever free.
Your wagging tails and eyes so bright,
In my heart, you shine with eternal light.

Though you've crossed the Rainbow Bridge,
Memories of you linger beyond the ridge.
The paw prints left on my very soul,
Testament of love that made me whole.

Thank you for the love and laughter,
Memories that will stay ever after.
You may be gone, yet memories are never erased,
Rest in peace, dear furry friends, in love's embrace.

I AM A TANKMAN, A MAN OF STEEL

(Pic of the author as Armoured Division Commander)

Being a Tankman was always a dream, a passion, and a destination for me. Many a time, I would go into a frenzy staring at Tanks displayed in Army Cantonments, imagining myself on one. This passion drew me to shun MBBS and join NDA. At IMA, I wrote all my choices as Armoured Corps and when hauled up, edited to fill only my first choice as Armoured Corps. The others were blank as it did not matter to me. Good fortune and merit got me my choice. Thereafter, destiny and toil took me from a Troop Leader to the Director General of Mechanised Forces over the next four decades. A blessed life journey of a Tankman.

'I Am a Tankman, A Man of Steel', is a spirited ode to the *'Men and Machines of the Armoured Corps'*. The narrative is a captivating exploration of the life and mindset of a Tankman, who embodies unwavering dedication, power, and adaptability. The tankman and his tank form an indomitable bond, conquering rugged terrains and battlefields with unmatched might. They command respect, leaving adversaries silenced and in awe. Amidst the dust and smoke, the Tankman's love for his machine is evident, creating a symphony of power and strength.

तू शहीं है पर्वाज़ है काम तेरा,
तेरे सामने आस्माँ और भी हैं,
सितारों से आगे जहाँ और भी हैं,
तेरे ज़मीन-ओ-मकाँ और भी हैं।

(Extracted from Iqbal's Couplet)

I Am a Tankman, A Man of Steel

I am a Tankman, a man of steel,
I ride the horse and drive the machine.
I pierce through virgin sand and snow,
I blaze the skies with an unmatched glow.

Tank my monster, crews my bonded pride,
In every battle, we ride side by side.
The dust and smoke our natural shroud,
Our enemies in awe, silenced and cowed.

I love the grease and champagne fuzz,
I create the music, my tracks' romantic buzz.
I enchant the damsels, tank fumes around,
I blaze the guns, romancing flash and sound.

I don't arrive; my arrival is announced,
I carry a swagger with bow legs pronounced.
I dance the salsa, tango's my game,
Winning hearts, stoking the flame.

I am God's creation, the master of beasts,
When I arrive, Satan's bow like priests.
My mission clear, to protect my flag and land,
My ferocity and courage my traditional brand.

May God have mercy on those who dare,
For I never forgive, forget, or ever spare.
Choice is yours to make way or kneel,
For I am a tankman, a man of steel.

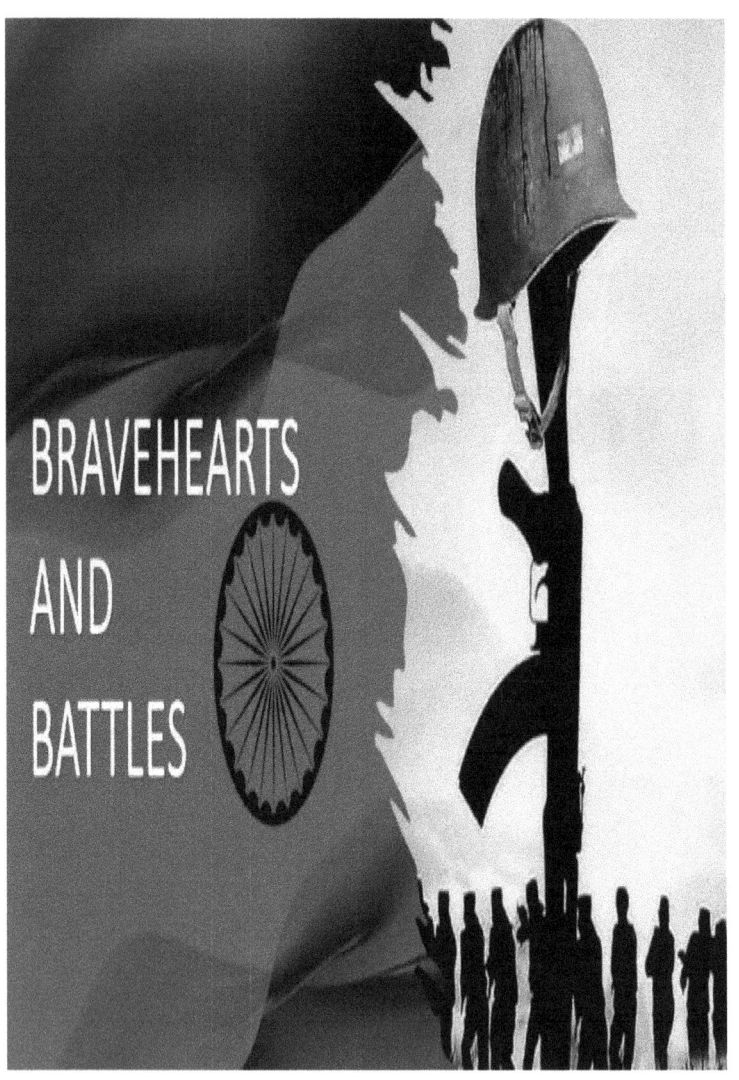

CHHATRAPATI SHIVAJI MAHARAJ: THE RADIANT LEGACY

(Pic courtesy – Jagranjosh.com)

Shivaji, a warrior of indomitable spirit and a visionary leader carved his name into the annals of history, embodying the essence of courage, resilience, and the relentless pursuit of sovereignty. The history of India is incomplete without mention of Chhatrapati Shivaji Maharaj, who established a powerful Hindu kingdom in southwestern India from 1642-1680. At just 16, he seized Torna fort, and by 17, Raigad and Kondana forts. A military genius and adept administrator, Shivaji's single-minded passion, unwavering integrity, courage, clear strategic vision, military prowess, and diplomacy created an independent kingdom against formidable foes. To quote Swami Vivekanand, *"Shivaji isn't just a name; it's an energy source for Indian youth striving for freedom."* My sister who is a historian often narrated to me vividly the stories of this great warrior whose exceptional leadership qualities have remained inspirational for me.

'Shivaji Maharaj: The Radiant Legacy' is my poetic tribute to the great Maratha warrior-king. The poem encapsulates Shivaji's remarkable life journey, from his youthful valour to his strategic brilliance in battles and conquests. It underlines Shivaji's unwavering commitment to justice, equality, and secularism, epitomising him as an icon of courage and leadership.

"जब हौसले बुलन्द हो,
तो पहाड़ भी एक मिट्टी का ढेर लगता है।"
.....छत्रपति शिवाजी महाराज

Chhatrapati Shivaji Maharaj: The Radiant Legacy

In annals of history, forever enshrined,
Chhatrapati Shivaji, a name so divine.
From youth, his valour a timeless stream,
In Sahyadri's embrace, destiny's beam.

Torna, Kondana, and Chakan, conquered in his prime,
Shivaji's bravery stood the test of time.
Against Bijapur's might, his banner did climb,
A threat to Adil Shah, victory his paradigm.

Strategies brilliant, his mind a star,
Leveraging geography, near and far.
Character, courage, in deeds that spar,
Equality and justice, his guiding North Star.

Champion of liberty, women's rights embraced,
Caste discrimination, he'd boldly defaced.
Tolerance for religions, all coexisted,
Secularism and justice, in his rule, enlisted.

Courage in our hearts, purpose in our stride,
In Shivaji's legacy, we'll forever take pride.
Through battles, trials, and storms that may arise,
We'll conquer every challenge, and reach the skies.

So let his spirit guide us, his values be our creed,
In every thought and action, every noble deed.
In the radiant legacy of Shivaji's illustrious might,
Find the strength to conquer, always do what's right.

ECHOES OF SARAGARHI: A TRIBUTE TO COURAGE

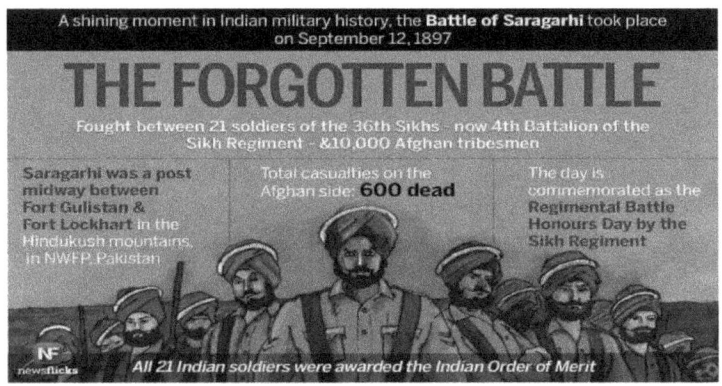

(Image courtesy -Disha Bharat)

The Battle of Saragarhi, fought on September 12, 1897, in the rugged Hindukush mountains of the North-West Frontier Province (now in Pakistan), is an inspiring event in the rich history of India. In the face of overwhelming odds, a mere 21 soldiers hailing from the British Indian Army's 36th Sikh Regiment, which is presently the Indian 4th Battalion of the Sikh Regiment, displayed extraordinary courage and fought with unwavering valour against a multitude of Afghan tribesmen. Their unyielding determination and gallantry stand as an enduring source of inspiration for generations to come. They sacrificed their lives but not before killing over 600

Afghan invaders. The Battle of Saragarhi will always be remembered as a shining example of courage and selfless sacrifice. It serves as an eternal inspiration for the soldier in me.

'*Echoes of Saragarhi: A Tribute to Courage*', is a poetic tribute that commemorates the historic battle of Saragarhi. The poem vividly portrays the heroic stand of twenty-one valiant soldiers who defended their post against overwhelming odds. The poem transcends time, echoing the valorous spirit of Saragarhi in the hearts of those who hear its verses. It calls on the youth of the nation, urging them to draw inspiration from Saragarhi's courage when facing challenges.

सरागढ़ी के वीर योद्धा, हमें देते संदेश यही,
वीरता और संघर्ष के साथ, जो भी लड़े, जीते वही।

Echoes of Saragarhi: A Tribute to Courage

September's twelfth, in eighteen ninety-seven,
Twenty-one souls rose like angels from heaven.
Ten thousand foes, a thunderous tide,
Yet these gallant warriors defended with pride.

In the cradle of courage, they stood as one,
Their hearts ablaze, their duty was done.
Loyalty to the core and the honour of the land,
Till last breath, they fought hand to hand.

Saragarhi's echoes forever will resound,
In the hearts of the brave, in history, unbound.
Twenty-one heroes, their sacrifice supreme,
In the annals of valour, an eternal dream.

When challenges loom, hope seems afar,
Remember Saragarhi, that shining star.
Hearts full of courage, they faced their fate,
A reminder to us, be brave, it's never too late.

Let their sacrifice remind you anew,
Strength and determination will see you through.
The battles you face, be they great or small,
Embrace them with passion, give it your all.

In unity and purpose, you shall find your way,
With every challenge, brighter comes the day.
So rise, O youth, with unwavering might,
In the name of Saragarhi, shine your light.

VALOUR AT HAIFA:
THE CAVALRY CHARGE

(Image – Battle of Haifa September 23, 1918)

The cavalry charge that unfolded in the Battle of Haifa during World War I is a striking testament to the remarkable bravery and prowess of the Indian cavalrymen. On September 23, 1918, the 15th Imperial Service Cavalry Brigade, consisting of troops from various regions in India, including Hyderabad, Mysore, and Jodhpur Lancers, played a pivotal role in this historic engagement. The brave Mysore Lancers and Jodhpur Lancers executed a daring charge against Ottoman forces in the coastal city of Haifa, which was held by the Turks. They captured 1,350 German and Ottoman prisoners, besides several weapons. Mounted on their trusty horses, these soldiers galloped fearlessly across the battlefield, overcoming formidable defences. One of the major losses that India experienced was that the Indian cavalry lost the 'Hero of Haifa' Major Dalpat Singh who earned his Military Cross that day. About 900 Indian soldiers are interred in cemeteries across Israel in Jerusalem, Ramle and Haifa. The sacrifice of Indian warriors in giving birth to other countries should be recorded in golden words in the pages of history.

The poem **'Valour at Haifa: The Cavalry Charge',** takes us to a time of gallant knights and their noble steeds, painting a lucid picture of courage and heroism on the battlefield. The poem pays tribute to the indomitable spirit of the Indian Cavalry and their legacy of honour and valour.

हाइफ़ा के मैदान में शौर्य का जज़्बा है यह,
कैवलरी के वीरों की बेमिसाल यादगार है यह।

Valour at Haifa: The Cavalry Charge

Banners held high, swords gleaming bright,
The cavalry charges, a thunderous sight.
On horseback, they ride, their sabres agleam,
Their courage and valour like a radiant beam.

Steads so robust, with pounding hooves,
Riders and horses, a partnership that proves.
In seamless grace, they move as one,
A bond of trust, battles to be won.

Through valleys and hills, they ride along,
The rhythm of gallop, a symphony's song.
Their discipline and training honed to perfection,
The cavalry's charge, a force of pure reflection.

With sabres drawn and lances set,
No foe can escape, no challenge they'd forget.
Their charge is swift, like lightning's fierce blaze,
The battlefield, their canvas, for honour and praise.

In days of yore, a history so vast,
The cavalry's legacy, forever cast.
Their valour and honour, an inspiration to all,
Duty's noble call, they'd rise standing tall.

In history's annals, Haifa's valour shall remain,
A beacon of bravery that will never wane.
With every charge, they wrote their tale,
In our hearts, their courage will forever prevail.

WAILS OF JALLIANWALA WALLS

(Pic of the bullet marks on the walls at Jallianwala Bagh)

The Jallianwala Bagh massacre (13 April 1919) in Amritsar remains a sombre chapter in India's struggle for independence from the oppressive British colonial rule. A large gathering of innocent Indians had assembled there to protest against the oppressive Rowlatt Act and the arrest of freedom fighters. The tragic event unfolded with General Reginald Dyer, a British officer, ordering his troops to fire indiscriminately. Dyer, without any warning, cruelly blocked the only exit and ordered his soldiers to fire indiscriminately at the men, women and children. This massacre resulted in the deaths of 379 people, with hundreds injured. The tragic event left a deep scar in the history of India and ignited widespread outrage and shock. It fuelled the ongoing freedom struggle. Ironically, karma had the last laugh as Gen Dyer suffered a series of strokes during the last years of his life and he became increasingly isolated due to the paralysis and speechlessness. He died of cerebral haemorrhage and arteriosclerosis on 23 July 1927.

The poem, **'Wails Of Jallianwala Walls',** poignantly captures the tragic events of the Jallianwala Bagh Massacre. It describes the haunting bullet marks on the walls, serving as a silent scar of the British brutality of that day. It also pays tribute to the brave people of India, their unity, and their unwavering spirit in the face of adversity, igniting a fire for freedom that would endure.

जलियांवाला बाग, जहाँ आज भी मासूम लोगों की चीखें सुनाई देती हैं,
जनरल डायर के अत्याचारों से दीवारें आज भी गुंज के रुला देती हैं।

Wails of Jallianwala Walls

Amritsar's heart, where history runs deep,
Tale of sorrow, where the walls still weep.
Bullet holes and bloodstains, a haunting display,
Reminiscence of Jallianwala Massacre, fateful day.

Rowlatt Act, a symbol of disdain,
Ignited a fire, a nation in pain.
Innocents gathered, seeking a peaceful voice,
Women and children, with no other choice.

Dyer's callous orders, slaughter untold,
Bullets rained, mercilessly behold.
Amidst the cries, the innocent fell,
Humanity bleeding, a sinister spell.

The walls still echo the anguished cries,
Of those who faced the fateful skies.
Men, women, children, in terror they fell,
A massacre so brutal, no tale can ever tell.

From this tragedy, a nation did rise,
Unity and strength reached the skies.
Sacrifice of those who never did bend,
Lit a fire of freedom that would never end.

Let us remember the Jallianwala Massacre's cost,
The lives that were taken, the innocence lost.
The spirit of a people who stood up tall,
And vowed to never let injustice befall.

ODE TO THE AZAD HIND FAUJ

(Image Courtesy – Wikimedia)

Some icons etch themselves into the annals of history, becoming everlasting idols. One such luminary is the true liberator and patriarch of India – Netaji Subhas Chandra Bose. He formed the provincial Govt. of Azad Hind and took oath as the first Prime Minister of undivided India in Singapore on 21 Oct 1943. Netaji's fervent brand of revolutionary patriotism reignited a dwindling flame of hope within the Indian freedom struggle, rekindling it after the suppression of the Quit India Movement from 1942 to 1945. I have always held this revered Indian hero in the highest regard, consistently highlighting his sacrifices and pivotal role in India's struggle for independence in my articles and talks. I firmly believe that the British colonial rulers were not solely compelled to retreat by the Quit India Movement, which was suppressed. Instead, it was the stimulus of the Azad Hind Fauj movement that led to a series of uprisings in February 1946, which left the British with no alternative but to leave India.

The poem, **'Ode to the Azad Hind Fauj',** pays tribute to these unsung heroes of India's struggle for independence—the soldiers of the Azad Hind Fauj. It highlights their sacrifices and love for the motherland that defined the independence struggle of India.

"कदम-कदम बढ़ाए जा, ख़ुशी के गीत गाए जा,
ये जिंदगी है क़ौम की, तू क़ौम पे लुटाए जा..."

(Indian Army marching tune based on Azad Hind Fauj Anthem)

Ode to the Azad Hind Fauj

In the struggle for India's independence, a saga unfolds,
Azad Hind Fauj, the forgotten army, history untold.
Turbulent year 1942, their freedom struggle arose,
Love for the motherland, blood and sacrifice flowed.

Epic slogan of "Jai Hind", the iconic salute of pride,
Rallying cry for the nation's epic freedom stride.
Unity, faith, and valour their motto glorified,
Mission first, warriors above gender unified.

The clarion call "Tum Mujhe Khoon Do",
The fearless promise "Mein Tumhe Azadi Dunga".
Pledge etched in courage and boundless devotion,
Igniting passion, spreading wild, across oceans.

Subhas Chandra Bose, a fierce leader locking horns,
Igniting the desire to martyr death, for India's dawn.
Men and women defying British oppressive might,
Hand in hand, the flame of freedom burning bright.

Freedom indeed came at a heavy price,
"Qadam Qadam Badaye Ja', unwavering sacrifice.
Each step a march toward India's morning sun,
Their untold saga, how independence was won.

So let us pledge to carry their eternal flame,
In our actions, we'll etch their revered name.
Fight all evil that divides our glorious land,
Above caste and religion, united we must stand.

BRAVE HEARTS OF INDIA'S FREEDOM STRUGGLE

Bhagat Singh   **Sukhdev**   **Rajguru**

(Image courtesy https://www.pinterest.com)

Bhagat Singh, Sukhdev Thapar, and Shivaram Rajguru, revered names etched in the annals of history, shook the foundations of the British Raj with their unwavering resolve. As they marched to the gallows, their smiles concealed the pain, for their love and sacrifice for the nation knew no bounds. They ignited a fire within the masses, uniting them in the fight for freedom. Their sacrifice reverberated across the nation with a resounding might that still echoes today. Their legacy endures as a timeless emblem of patriotism. Their words, etched in history, remind us that ideas are invincible, and life is lived on its own terms. Their courage and valour stand as a testament to our shared pride. Their sacrifice serves as a perpetual reminder of our duty: to protect and respect the principles for which they gave their lives. As a child, I often heard tales of their bravery from my father, who was also a college-day freedom fighter. These poems serve as a reflection of those cherished moments that have left a profound mark on my soul.

The poem **'Brave Hearts of India's Freedom Struggle'**, pays homage to these iconic and highlights their unwavering dedication to their nation. The poem underscores their ability to inspire and unite the masses in the fight for freedom and portrays their courageous stance against oppressive colonial power. It serves as an enduring reminder of their profound contribution to India's struggle for independence and the solemn responsibility to honour their sacrifice.

"जिंदगी तो अपने दम पर जी जाती है,
दूसरों के कंधों पर तो सिर्फ़ जनाज़े उठाए जाते हैं।"
.......शहीद भगत सिंह

Brave Hearts of India's Freedom Struggle

Bhagat Singh, Sukhdev Thapar and Shivaram Rajguru,
Names in our glorious history that shook the British Raj.
Marched to the gallows with smiles on their face,
Love and sacrifice for the nation they bravely embraced.

Youthful and zealous, they carried freedom's torch,
Uniting the masses, igniting a powerful scorch.
Against colonial tyranny, they stood hand in hand,
Their sacrifice echoes through time, and across the land.

For their beloved land's freedom, they fiercely fought,
Against oppression and cruelty, they valiantly sought.
With unwavering resolve and spirits so grand,
Their legacy endures a sublime, eternal brand.

Their ideals persist, an everlasting breath,
Their words defy death, conquering even its depth.
"They may kill me," they said, their voices ringing wide,
"But not our ideas, nor the spirit we stride."

In the heart of every Indian, their memory lives,
A reminder of what sacrifice and dedication give.
They taught us to cherish the freedom we've earned,
In their honour, our unity is forever affirmed.

So let us remember these heroes, forever in our hearts,
Their bravery and sacrifice, a beacon that imparts.
The spirit of a nation, independence as we celebrate,
These heroes of the nation, we shall ever commemorate.

ODE TO GALLANT HORSEMEN AND TANKMEN

(Collage by the Author)

The *'Armoured Corps'* evolved from the cavalry when horses were replaced by Tanks in the 20th Century. The history of the Indian Armoured Corps is a rich heritage of the elan and a saga of blood, courage, and chivalry. I got commissioned in the 7th Light Cavalry in Dec 1978, a Regiment raised in 1784 and with numerous battle and theatre honours. The Regiment too transited with honour from Cavalry to a Tank Regiment. Both the Horsemen and Tankmen of this illustrious Regiment have won several gallantry awards and brought glory to the nation and the Regiment. I owe my upbringing to this Regiment and dedicate this poem to the Horsemen and Tankmen of the 7th Light Cavalry.

'Ode to Gallant Horsemen and Tankmen', celebrates the fearless spirit of traditional Cavalrymen and contemporary Tankmen. The poem vividly captures the cavalry charge as a thrilling rush of adrenaline, a saga of courageous might. Transitioning to modern times, the poem introduces tankmen, who inherit the same ferocity and courage as their ancestral counterparts. They are the knights of today, roaring engines and blazing guns, conquering deserts, and fiery battlegrounds with equal pride.

**तू शाहीन है, परवाज़ है तेरा काम,
घोड़ सवार से टैंक सवार, जिन्होंने पाया यह नाम,
रोक नहीं सकता कोई तुझको, ज़मीन या आसमान,
तू कुदरत का फ़रिश्ता है, तेरा है यह जहान।**

Ode to Gallant Horsemen and Tankmen

Thunderous hooves, the chivalrous charge,
Echoing war cries, dust plumes enlarge.
Galloping horses, fearlessness strides,
Clouding sky, ruling earth with arrogant pride.

The cavalry charge, a sight to behold,
A rush of adrenaline, a story to be told.
Sabres unleashed, lances ripping, tearing all apart,
The cavalry charge, saga of horses and brave hearts.

Rolled in the mighty tanks, a spirit of the past,
Roaring engines, blazing guns, armour cast.
Charger or tank, horsemen, or tankmen,
Ferocity defines the spirit, courage of Iron Man.

Rumbling tanks, a modern-day knight,
Rule the deserts to fiery heights.
Heritage unforgotten they adapt to times,
Winning damsels and battles with equal pride.

In history's annals, their valour engraved,
From gallant horsemen to tanks that paved.
Legends and heroes, strong and true,
To gallant horsemen and tankmen, we salute you!

We bow our heads and honour their sacrifice,
Horsemen to tankmen who gave their lives.
Through mud and blood, they blazed a path,
We follow with pride, their memory steadfast.

CELEBRATING INDIA'S FREEDOM SYMPHONY

(Image Courtesy Kindpng)

India's struggle for independence was a heroic and unwavering battle against British colonial rule that spanned decades. It was marked by non-violent protests, civil disobedience, and sacrifices by several heroes of the nation, some through armed struggle too. The numerous sacrifices by ordinary Indians exemplified the nation's fervour for freedom. On August 15, 1947, India finally achieved its long-awaited independence, a momentous day that marked the end of colonial oppression and the dawn of a new era, when the tricolour was hoisted, and the nation took its first steps towards a vibrant democracy.

'Celebrating India's Freedom Symphony', is a poetic tribute to India's Independence Day, encapsulating the essence of the nation's journey to freedom and its diverse cultural tapestry. The poem highlights the soaring spirit of the day, paying homage to the epic struggle for liberty led by iconic figures like Gandhi, Netaji, Bhagat Singh, and Rani Jhansi. It also recognizes the sacrifices of the armed forces in safeguarding the borders and preserving its independence. It finally gives a call for unity, equality, and the dissolution of divides among its citizens, promoting the idea of 'Nation Above All' and collective nation-building.

आज लहरायेगा तिरंगा हमारा,
वादियों की जन्नत से समुंदर की लहरों के साथ,
एक नया अल्फ़ाज़, एक नया जज़्बात,
एक भारत - एक तिरंगा - एक सीरत के साथ।

Celebrating India's Freedom Symphony

Celebrating Independence Day, spirit soar high,
Symphony of freedom, the anthem echoing the sky.
With pride, we salute the tricolour, the epic fight,
A nation was born today, in liberty's radiant light.

In vibrant hues of diversity, the idea of India unfurls,
A land where ancient tales and dreams softly whirl.
Himalayan peaks to sun-kissed shores, nation's pride,
With tolerance and harmony, India's rich culture resides.

Gandhi's nonviolence, to Netaji's epic fight,
Mangal Pandey leading, Bhagat Singh's sacrifice.
Azad's freedom struggle to Rani Jhansi's clarion call,
Unsung heroes inspire, India's canvas stands tall.

Freedom earned at a cost, many challenges anew unfold,
Warriors brave and bold, spirit of 'Nation Above All' retold.
Soldiers guarding frontiers, their valour untold,
Today's sacrifice, tomorrow's hope they uphold.

Let unity and equality, bridge the manmade divides,
Love and respect, as the strengths of the nation's pride.
In peaceful harmony, let us stand united as one,
Let differences dissolve, our unity challenged by none.

Nation building above all, is our collective goal,
From villages to cities, let the story of Bharat unfold.
As we march to the future, let this rekindle the flame,
21st Century – the Indian Century, we proudly acclaim.

ZOJILA 1948 -
THE SAVIOUR OF LADAKH

(Pic Courtesy 7th Light Cavalry)

I have had the honour of being commissioned in the illustrious **7th Light Cavalry** of Zojila Fame. The Battle of Zojila epitomizes one of the greatest battles in the annals of military history which ensured that Ladakh became an inseparable part of Indian geography. This battle saw the audacious use of Stuart light tanks by the Regiment, a feat that defied the odds of rugged terrain and high altitude of 11,575 feet. The pass's perilous conditions, including avalanches and extreme temperatures, made the build-up of tanks most challenging, including the ingenious camouflage of tanks as trucks to maintain secrecy and the most innovative dismantling turrets to traverse the bridges and passes. The Battle of Zojila Pass paved the way for the liberation of Ladakh and serves as a testament to the indomitable spirit of the Indian Army.

The poem *'Zojila 1948 – The Saviour of Ladakh'*, recounts the gripping story of the capture of Zojila Pass, and the heroic efforts of Indian forces, to secure victory against formidable odds. This poem is dedicated to the 7th Light Cavalry, the Saviours of Ladakh.

जोजीला की वह चोटी, नामुमकिन दास्तान,
टैंकों ने दिया बुलंद जवाब आलीशान,
गुमरी में टैंक की परछाईं एक खौफनाक नज़ारा,
भागा दुश्मन, डर और खौफ से मारा मारा।

Zojila 1948 - The Saviour of Ladakh

1948, Kashmir's destiny teetered on the edge,
Ladakh's future hung from a fragile ledge.
With bold enemy forces poised to strike,
Leh besieged, a tale concealed from sight.

Zojila Pass, a treacherous gateway to defend,
Guarding Ladakh's fate, where hopes blend.
The adversary held it with all his might,
Guns poised, ready for the relentless fight.

Infantry charged, their valour on display,
Yet Zojila's grip, they couldn't sway.
Stuart tanks, our nation's last resort,
Seventh Cavalry mission impossible sought.

At dawn on November's first, tension swelled,
Artillery roared, skies with fire compelled.
Tanks surged through Zojila, engines roared,
At Gumri basin, the winds of victory soared.

Incredulous, the enemy stood in fear,
Tanks at heights, imagination never near.
Demoralised, they fled, their panic clear,
Victory resounded brave hearts in cheer.

In the pursuit of dreams, on uncharted roads,
Harness your potential, and break all the codes.
Embrace challenges, let your ambitions soar,
Let Zojila's spirit flame your hearts evermore.

GUARDIANS OF THE TRICOLOUR

(Image Courtesy – The Print)

The Indian Army, the nation's last bastion is an institution with a rich and historic legacy. It stands as a shining and proud example of professionalism and valour. Rooted in a tradition of service that dates back centuries, it embodies the highest standards of discipline, commitment, and gallantry. Through time immemorial, it has stood as the last bastion of the nation's honour with unparalleled dedication. In peacetime, their contribution to nation-building activities exemplifies their dedication to the welfare of the citizens they protect. The Indian Army is a symbol of India's pride, strength, and unity. As the Indian Army continues to stand guard, it upholds the honour of the tricolour with every step, carrying forward a legacy of valour and dedication. I salute my Alma mater.

'Guardians of the Tricolour', is a tribute to the indomitable spirit and utmost commitment of the Indian Army. It portrays the saga of valour and sacrifices of these Bravehearts who stand as the nation's guardians. The poem encapsulates their courage, duty, and unbreakable bond with the tricolour, inviting us to reflect upon the deep respect and gratitude we owe to these selfless protectors of our nation.

"या तो मैं तिरंगा फहराने के बाद वापस आऊंगा, या फिर मैं इसी में लिपटकर वापस आऊंगा, लेकिन मैं निश्चित रूप से वापस आऊंगा।"
- कैप्टन विक्रम बत्रा, PVC(P)

Guardians of The Tricolour

In the land where legends are born,
A force emerges, brave and adorned.
The Indian Army, a source of pride,
Service Before Self, their motto to abide.

A saga unfolds, countless sacrifices untold,
Valiant hearts, in adversity's stronghold.
Men and women warriors, spirits enshrined,
Marching through the storms, courage aligned.

From deserts to plains, jungles to icy peaks,
Enduring every battle, courage never weak.
Standing tall, defending the nation's honour,
Fighting for freedom and peace with fervour.

Born to fight, trained to kill,
Prepared to die, their duty they fulfil.
On the battlefield, mercy has no creed,
Every adversity, they strive to succeed.

Naam, Namak, and Nishan, in their veins run true,
Regimental izzat, a sacred oath they pursue.
Comrades in arms, marching with pride,
Till their last breath, the tricolour beside.

In the heart of the nation, forever they dwell,
Indian Army, Nation's pride, our hearts swell.
May our gratitude and respect forever shine,
For their service to the nation's sacred line.

THE LOVE OF UNIFORM

(Pic of the Authors Medals)

Born into a lineage of soldiers, the hue of olive green adorned every season and became a way of life. Unfortunately, it was not the era of women in uniform or else there would have been many more in the family. The textures of the uniform changed from starched cotton to teri-cotton and so did the service dress from Sam Browns to Olive Green. Yet the joy of donning the uniform with stars on the shoulders and medals on the chest was unparalleled. Though the number of medals I earned might have measured up to my father's, the quality of his war medals surpassed mine, making them treasures of unparalleled significance. Given an opportunity to choose my destiny in the next life and ever thereafter, the uniform would remain my first love.

'The Love of Uniform', is a poem that celebrates the profound devotion and unwavering dedication of individuals who wear the uniform in service to their nation. It encapsulates the essence of a soldier's life, highlighting the symbolism of medals, the nobility of the path chosen, and the deep bonds formed among comrades. It underscores the sacrifices endured and the unwavering spirit that propels those who dedicate themselves to service, portraying a vivid image of a life in uniform as an enduring, fervent commitment.

>
> कंधे पर चमकता हुआ एक तारा,
> सारे जहां से जगमगाता प्यारा।
> वर्दी मेरी जान है,
> देश की यह शान है।

The Love of Uniform

A star on the shoulder shining bright,
Better than a million on the starlit night.
Love for the uniform, a flame so bright,
Burning within with unwavering might.

Upon the chest, tales of valour reside,
Every medal a chapter, courage side by side.
Proud lifetime weaved in metal so fine,
Saga of courage and sacrifice enshrined.

Soldiering a life, noble and revered,
Chosen by hearts undaunted, undeterred.
Vows of sacrifice, even life, they make,
For the nation's love, they pave the way.

Leaders forged in this crucible's fire,
Guiding with courage, never to tire.
Upholding the nation's honour, standing tall,
Meeting challenges, their clarion call.

Life in uniform, a blessing unfurled,
Path exclusive to the bravest in the world.
Comrades bonded, thicker than blood,
Lifelong, in unity, their emotions flood.

If in life's to come, I could choose my design,
A path forever of warrior, so truly divine.
With boundless passion, soul, and mind,
Dedicated to the Nation, no better honour to find.

A TRIBUTE TO MY TANKMEN MENTORS

(Veteran's All - Risaldar Honorary Captain Risal Singh and Risaldar Honorary Captain Hoshiyar Singh with the author)

Some of life's memories remain evergreen and blessings eternal. One such memory was of my days in Jan of 1979 when I joined the 7th Light Cavalry at Jammu on my first posting. As the baby of the Regiment, called Mr Ashok Shivane (Rank was only restored after credibility with men and Young Officer's course completed), I lived with my tank crew of No 2 Troop A squadron in their lines. A tank was given on my charge to learn to master it and maintain it. My Troop Dafadar Ram Singh, and Senior JCO Hony Capt. then Ris Hawa Singh put me through the inside out of the tank till I resembled more of a 'Greaseman than a Tankman'. Life revolved around the bonding of man and machine.

Yet it would not have been possible but for those unsung heroes who made me a Tankman. They remain my Gurus bonded for life.

This Poem is a tribute to my Tankmen mentors. I owe my professional career to these men of Steel who grounded me in the world of tank and tank warfare.

टैंक के साथ मिलकर टैंकमैन का सुहाना सफर,
2nd लेफ्टिनेंट से जनरल तक, वर्दी का यह सफर।
गुरुओं की सिखाई का आभार, मेरे दिल का बयां,
उनके बिना जीवन का सफर, एक अधूरी दास्तान।

A Tribute to My Tankmen Mentors

To those Tankmen, with wisdom and men of steel,
Who nurtured the subaltern, with profound zeal.
They made me toil in mud and sweat every day,
Taught me to master the tank, come what may.

Grease-stained dungarees and mucky face with pride,
Mastering each tank part, with them by my side.
In peace, they said, the bond we'd fortify,
So, in battle, my tank would never belie.

They instilled in me the art of shoot to kill,
To strike first, before foes could hone their skill.
Storms and narrow bridges, made me drive,
Under their watchful eyes, our bond would thrive.

Tank crew they stressed, a bond of might,
Honing our skills through day and night.
To these tankmen, my mentors, so grand,
Salute you Sirs for moulding my stand.

In the realm of armour, where metal meets might,
I owe my mettle to those who guided me right.
From a young subaltern to a General's role,
Their foundation endures in my Tankman's soul.

As time rolls on, now veterans we stand,
The bond of love and respect, hand in hand.
Through the years, our souls intertwined,
In the tapestry of life, a lifelong blessing enshrined.

THE CRADLE OF MILITARY LEADERSHIP

(Pic Courtesy – Indianpolitics.co.in)

The nostalgia of National Defence Academy (NDA) days cannot be defined. It remains vivid and occupies a plethora of countless memories. The arrival marked lifting steel trunks on the head followed by a crew cut in the days when sidelocks and long hair were the fashion of the day. In the hustle and bustle that followed, we woke up for PT and drill, ate 15 toasts, carried another five in satchel and went to classes with bikes on our shoulders only to sleep with our eyes open. Of course, memories of a school girl who used to cross our path at 7.10 am and the liberty (outing) at Pune coffee house and Sizzlers, watching pretty damsels remain evergreen. 'Tipsy Gadar', the hijacking of tipsy pudding after each training camp and filling them in mess tins was an art. Then there was a famous horse we rode who seemed intoxicated biting the front horse's backside neighing, which remained a nightmare. Between the Divisional Officer (Divo) and Drill Ustad, we picked up our vocabulary. Those were the days my friends with whom we remain bonded for life.

This poem **'The Cradle of Military Leadership',** is an emotional tribute to the National Defence Academy (NDA), where the metamorphosis of young cadets into fearless warriors takes place. It is of the bygone days as many things have changed now, especially with the welcome induction of girls to NDA. The poem portrays some defining humorous moments in my journey and finally salutes the heroes who find their resting place in the 'Halls of Fame'.

कुछ यादें, कुछ बातें, यादें रह जाती हैं,
कुछ खूबसूरत पलों की महक रह जाती हैं।

The Cradle of Military Leadership

In the cradle of leadership, dreams take flight,
NDA, forging men from boys, who shine bright.
Through rigorous training, an endurance of might,
Bodies pushed beyond limits, minds new heights.

Crew cuts, a mark of unity, we wore with pride,
In Pune girls' eyes, naughty smiles, side by side.
Adventure of restrictions, escapes on liberty's tide,
Drill Ustad's shouts, many a metaphor still resides.

Torches on the chests, enlightened we'd proclaim,
Crossing the 7.10 Girl on cycles, all thinking the same.
Movies in the auditorium, dreams of blissful rest,
Woken for front rolls, everything topsy turvy at best.

Scaling peaks, named after actress's anatomical fame,
Post-dinner "fall-ins," outcomes known all the same.
Anteroom parade, Bonny M, Abba's sweet sway,
John Travolta's moves in our dance steps did stay.

Horses that disobey, cadets astride a sight,
Cabins meant for sleep, yet awake all night.
Meals by the minutes, oh what a gigantic appetite,
Tipsy pudding 'Gadar', mess tins overflowing, a sight.

In the hallowed 'Halls of Fame', many a heroes rest,
A place where courage and grit don the brave's chest.
NDA our Alma Mater, our motto 'Service Before Self',
Bonded for life, our hearts and chests with pride swell.

WE ARE GOLFIES, CAN'T YOU SEE

(Pic by Author of a camp in NDA with his coursemates)

In January 1975, I became a part of NDA's Golf Squadron. Among the 12 squadrons, Golf was most notorious for its demanding tough and unforgettable experiences. As first-term cadets on a six-term journey, we spent more time carrying our bicycles than riding them. Those were the days we were made to hang from *'Seventh Heaven'* (the seventh wire strand on the ventilator above the cabin door). Our nights were often in solace beneath the staircase, not in bed to avoid front rolls. Each evening brought an anteroom parade, and first-termers had their unique curtain raiser during the Intro Night. Those days were defined by starched Khaki Drill attire and Drill Instructors who pushed us to our limits. Punishments, known as *'restrictions',* were doled out generously. It was a time of *"Never say why, but to do or die."* Those were the days of bonding, my friend!

The poem **'We Are Golfies, Can't You See'**, takes the reader on a nostalgic journey through the bonds and memories forged among friends in the NDA's Golf squadron. The verses vividly depict the camaraderie and unity shared by the group as they navigated their youthful days together. Through restrictions and secret moments, it captures the essence of a lifetime of cherished memories.

वोह थी गोल्फ स्क्वाड्रन की यारी,
जिसने दी थी हमारी रूह को रुस्तगारी।
वो सुनहरे दिन, वो सुनहरी रातें,
अब रह गईं इस बंधन की बातें।

We Are Golfies, Can't You See

Those were the days my lovely friends,
We forged a lifetime, bonded till the end.
NDA's Golf squadron, buddies side by side,
A life where boundless memories reside.

Together we rolled, ran and played,
In the anteroom, intro nights a parade.
With bikes on shoulders, and toasts in hand,
Through youthful days, we traversed the land.

On the drill square, marching with pride,
Many a time, by the double, side by side.
To Sinhgad's heights, we hiked all weather,
Restrictions the name, flocks all together,

Beneath the staircase's shadowed space,
We rested our heads in that secret place.
In silent moments, many a breath to hold,
Pulled out, made to roll, memories behold.

Bathing in unity, camaraderie so pure,
Our KD shorts pulled, in jest and more.
Seventh heaven, recollection of the past,
Lifetime frozen memories, forever to last.

As the sun sets and welcomes dawn's first ray,
We stand firm as Golfies, come what may.
Singing, "Chikki Lakka, Bamboo Lakka, Who are we?"
Shouting back "We are Golfies, Can't you see!"

WORLD OF ARMY ANECDOTES

(Pic of Author with armour course mates during Young Officers Course 1979- Refer Anecdote 3)

In the world of army anecdotes, we find cherished memories that we celebrate and toast with champagne in our blessed lifetimes. These stories forever tether us to the splendid days of yore. I too have my share of mystic anecdotes.

Anecdote 1: As a young, newly commissioned second lieutenant with only a few months of service in the regiment, I was appointed Train Adjutant of C Squadron (Sikhs) in the 7th Light Cavalry. The regiment was on a permanent move from Kaluchak to Babina, travelling in an exquisite rail wagon called 'Flats' (a plain, flat tank carrier bogey). The freshness of the strong February breeze on the tank deck was heavenly. The military train felt like a private conveyance, with the driver and guard won over by generous rations of rum. One motivated soldier, Mukund Singh, suddenly ordered the train to halt as it passed through his village. So, we stopped for fresh *'sarson ka saag'* and *'makki ki roti,'* served with copious amounts of homemade white butter and *'lassi'* for all. The next scheduled stop was at Karnal's outer line. However, as the train was about to resume its journey from Karnal, it was halted by Railway Police claiming that a goat had been taken aboard. My Troop Dafadar Inderjit Singh vehemently denied this and challenged them to inspect the entire train. A thorough search was conducted, but nothing was found. Consequently, the train was allowed to continue its journey. That evening, we were treated to a lavish dinner of mutton curry, despite it not being in the designated menu of the day. I inquired about the source of the mutton from Inderjit. Later, the mystery over rum was unveiled—it was the missing goat, cleverly concealed inside a bag of wheat to muffle its cries and disguise its shape. It was an ingenious ruse, and we all shared a hearty laugh over roti, mutton curry, and our designated two tots of rum.

Anecdote 2: Upon arriving in Babina, a typical day was filled with physical training from 6 am to 7 am, followed by duties on the tank, clad in black dungarees, until lunch. In the evenings, we engaged in activities like cycle polo and troop games, before concluding the day at the Mess for our evening drinks and dinner. The time between cycle polo and dinner was often spent driving around the arid landscape of Babina or venturing to Jhansi Railway Colony and Girls College during weekends, where tankmen had ample opportunities for flirting and dancing. Nights were peaceful and restful. One hot summer night in 1979, in a bachelor's room, a large, old MES ceiling fan decided to fall onto my bed, just below where I lay. I had returned from Jhansi late on a Sunday night and must have been enjoying a particularly vivid dream, as my legs were sprawled wide apart. The impact of the fan, sandwiched between my legs, caused me to sit up abruptly on the bed in sheer disbelief for a few seconds. But the dream was too precious to abandon, so I settled back down, with the fan's central hub still nestled between my legs and its wings resting on my shins. My buddy, Chamkaur Singh, came the next morning to wake me with tea at 5:30 a.m. To his horror, he saw me sound asleep with the fan still in that peculiar position. He exclaimed, *'Sahib Ji!'* I awoke to the realization of the night's bizarre episode. Later that day, I was taken to the Gurudwara Sahib to offer my gratitude for escaping such an extraordinary mishap miraculously.

Anecdote 3: The first significant milestone in an army officer's journey is the Young Officers Course (YO's), marking the official designation of a Second Lieutenant. The YO's course is also a lot of fun as it's the first time officers from the same arm come together. One of my dear coursemates during the YO's course fell in love (unilaterally) with the Wing Commander's daughter, who was in her final year of school. Her father, a conservative and protective officer, was seldom seen, and we encountered them only during open-air movie screenings at the Ahmednagar military club known as 'Annexe.' Until then, my coursemates had exchanged only affectionate glances and shy smiles with the girl, who responded with limited acknowledgement. Bringing them together was a seemingly impossible mission, and I was entrusted with the task by my coursemates. We devised a plan: I would host a birthday celebration in mid-October (even though my actual birthday is on December 13th) and invite the instructor along with his family. The mission was to keep the family engaged while my course mate-initiated contact with the girl, breaking the ice. The stage was set, and I extended a convincing invitation to the Colonel Instructor and his family for my cake-cutting ceremony at the Mess. After some hesitation, he agreed to attend for a brief while. Thus, he, his wife, his son and, most importantly, his daughter attended the celebration. The plan worked, and my coursemates successfully introduced himself to the girl and exchanged greetings. A memorable pic was also taken with the girl, her brother and our gang of rogues. Ironically, a few days later, the instructor discovered that my actual birthday was in December. What unfolded thereafter is another story best left forgotten, but the mission was accomplished, albeit with some consequences.

Anecdote 4: It was the first Holi celebration after the YO's course in Babina. Before the course, my parents had gifted me a blue Yezdi motorcycle. In a playful spirit, I decided to invert the 'YEZDI' brand plate, transforming it into 'IDZEY.' IDZEY soon became Tankman's love and talk of the town. Came Holi a festival of colours, joy, and dance, so the festivities began with a celebration with my squadron men. We indulged in rum, danced, and painted each other beyond recognition with vibrant colours. After an hour of revelry, we headed to the Brigade Mess, where Bhang Pakoras served as delectable appetizers, accompanied by Bhang drink at its purest. Finally, we returned to our own Regimental Officers Mess, where beer flowed freely, and tandoori chicken was served. The mixing of drinks became more colourful than the hues on our faces. Amidst the festivities, I had promised to drop my immediate senior, Kamal, at the Babina railway station (5 km away) to catch a train at 13:25, as he was heading home on casual leave. Time passed swiftly, but the vow between brother officers to fulfil the commitment remained unbroken. It was now 13:45. The train had already departed at 13:40. Kamal, being more composed than me, reminded me that because of me he missed the train. This hit the heart. A Tankman's promise is most honourable, so I made Kamal sit on my IDZEY with his bag and to his utter dismay rode cross country alongside the railway track from Babina to Jhansi, assuring him that I would ensure he boarded the same train. Kamal's more than bumpy journey was filled with his choicest vocabulary, the echoes of which remained unheard. About 15 kilometres short of Jhansi, near the BHEL Factory, the train had come to a halt due to a signal. It was at this point that I caught up with the train and safely deposited Kamal into the train. Mission accomplished, promise honoured, yet Kamal was in shock. Even years later, when we meet, we still raise a toast to these unforgettable and amusing memories.

> *"बस यादें, यादें, यादें रह जाती हैं*
> *छोटी, छोटी, बातें रह जातीं हैं*
> *बस यादें......................"*

World of Army Anecdotes

In memories old, where stories flow,
Anecdotes of army life aglow.
With laughter ringing, hearts so light,
Nostalgic memories, a soldier's delight.

In dusty boots and black dungaree attire,
We faced each day, never to tire.
From early reveille to lights-out late,
We marched through life, comrades so great.

Remember that time in the pouring rain,
Mud-soaked uniforms, a comical terrain.
We slipped and slid, couldn't stay upright,
But in those muddy moments, spirits took flight.

Late night guard checks under starry skies,
Exaggerated love stories, oh, those lies!
We'd amaze each other, then laugh till dawn,
In the army, such memories are drawn.

Nostalgia paints the colours of the past,
In shades of humour, the memories cast.
Though we've moved on, those days are gold,
In the annals of army life, many a story retold.

So, here's to the army, the laughter we shared,
The anecdotes and memories, feelings cared.
With laughter and grins, we couldn't resist,
Tales of camaraderie with a comical twist.

KARGIL: THE HOME OF IMMORTAL BRAVES

(Image Courtesy – The Times of India)

The Kargil War an armed conflict, was deceitfully waged by Pakistan at extreme altitudes ranging from 15,000 to 18,000 feet of Kargil district in Jammu and Kashmir. The courageous Indian soldiers engaged Pakistani forces masquerading as intruders, having breached the Line of Control into Indian territory. This fierce struggle endured from May 8, 1999, to July 26, 1999, culminated in India's triumph as they successfully repelled the Pakistani Army. As a young Lieutenant Colonel handling the Internal Security (Counter Terrorism) desk in Srinagar, I witnessed first-hand the initial sparks that heralded the Kargil War, which soon flared, necessitating the rapid deployment of troops to confront the crisis. My perspective of this war unfolded from a staff desk, where I bore witness to the valour of our brave soldiers and the poignant arrival of numerous body bags via helicopters. My salute to these valiant souls. The victory achieved against formidable odds is a testament to the indomitable prowess of the Indian Army.

'Kargil: The Home of Immortal Braves', is an emotive poem crafted to pay homage to the unwavering courage, sacrifice, and indomitable spirit of the brave Indian soldiers who fought in the Kargil War. This poem captures the very essence of the conflict that unfurled in the unforgiving Himalayan terrain, where heroes emerged from the crucible of adversity and secured victory for our nation.

भारत के हैं हम वीर जवान,
कारगिल की हैं हम शान,
हर चोटी पर लिखी हमारी बुलंदी,
देश के इतिहास में हमारा सुनहरा नाम।

Kargil: The Home of Immortal Braves

In the Himalayas, where icy peaks stand tall,
Lies Kargil, the home of Braves last clarion call.
Midst of chilling winds, where snow and silence meet,
Echoes the courage of those who fought without retreat.

Shattering the peace, a cowardly plot untold,
Tales of deceit, as Operation Koh Paima unfolds.
Cloaked as mujahideen, Paki soldiers crept in guise,
But young Indian soldiers stood tall, defying the lies.

The treacherous heights, where silence speaks,
Echoed with valour, blooding the icy peaks.
With bullets and shells, the valleys did grieve,
Yet they stood firm, not an inch of land to concede.

Amidst the fury, countless heroes willingly plunged,
Families prayed, hearts ached, yet hopes clung.
Their saga of sacrifice, brave sons ever so young,
Fearless they fought all for the nation, yet unsung.

The war of Kargil holds lessons profound,
For the future, let modernisation be sound.
With a resolve to be prepared and wise,
To win our battles with lesser cost of lives.

Oh, dear citizens, united we must stand,
To honour the braves who freed our land.
Respect the families who bear a lifelong scar,
Salute the Indian Army, the Nation's shining star.

BRAVEHEARTS OF GALWAN

(Photo Credit – India Today)

In May 2020, the remote Galwan Valley in the Himalayas witnessed a dramatic escalation in the long-standing border dispute between India and China. The world watched in awe as a violent confrontation unfolded on the night of June 15, resulting in casualties on both sides – thwarting the Chinese nefarious plan. Amidst this perilous situation, Indian soldiers displayed extraordinary courage and valour, engaging in hand-to-hand combat with their Chinese counterparts who came equipped with crude weapons.

'Bravehearts of Galwan', is a poignant poem that pays homage to the unsung heroes, the soldiers at Galwan who stalled the Chinese incursion in defense of their homeland. The verses vividly capture the courage, sacrifice, and indomitable spirit of these brave soldiers, unwavering in their commitment to safeguarding the nation's freedom and glory. It also delivers a resounding message to those who threaten peace, underlining that evil hands can never extinguish the valorous flames of those who defend our land.

अमर रहें वीर सैनिक गलवान के,
देश की रक्षा की, जिन्होंने अपनी जान से,
चीन को सिखाया सबक इन्हीं बलवानों ने,
तिरंगे को लहराया, इन्होंने गलवान में।

Bravehearts of Galwan

*You braved the killer winds with soldierly grace,
Confronted the enemy's storm in your embrace.
You smiled in the face of death's eerie song,
Saluting the Tri-colours, brave and strong.*

*In trenches deep and mountains high,
Your bravery and valour touched the sky.
Guardians unwavering, resolute, and bold,
Defending our land, your stories remain untold.*

*In the face of danger, your courage never waned,
A hero's sacrifice, forever in history's frame.
For you signed a bond with no expiry,
Inked in blood, valour, and nation's glory.*

*I am no hero, but have walked alongside many,
Felt the soldier's last breath, a poignant journey.
Witnessed the families in anguish and despair,
Soldiers facing death, a world sheltered, unaware.*

*Be not proud those blood-stained killer hands,
You can never silence the saviours of our lands.
You've only marked yourself with evil's brand,
You shall pay the price; you will never withstand.*

*Hey, countrymen, spare a moment, please,
No bells, no noise, no torches to appease.
Just a solemn candle, a prayer to unroll,
Saluting brave hearts and immortal souls.*

BALIDAAN :
ODE TO THE BRAVE HEARTS OF RAJOURI

(Pic of the Balidaan Emblem)

The Kesari Hills in Kandi, Rajouri, bore witness to a tragic chapter in our nation's ongoing battle against terrorism on 5th May 2023. Five elite para commandos of the Army's Special Forces, true heroes in every sense, laid down their lives in the line of duty. These brave souls were on a mission, a specific operation aimed at combating the menace of militancy. The militants were subsequently hounded and gunned down. This encounter serves as a stark reminder of the daunting challenges our armed forces face and the importance of ongoing efforts to counter terrorism in maintaining peace in the region. The nation must salute these real heroes who laid down their lives. Their sacrifice must forever inspire us to stand united against those who threaten our national security.

The poem **'Balidaan: Ode to The Brave Hearts of Rajouri',** paints a poignant picture of courage and sacrifice amidst the challenging terrain of Rajouri's hills. As cowards strike from the shadows, promising lives are cut short, but the fallen heroes' sacrifice fuels a relentless pursuit of justice. The poem pays rich tribute to these brave warriors and their families. It affirms the resolve to carry on the fight against terror.

राजौरी की पहाड़ियों में वीरता के अफ़साने,
वहीं उठते हैं बहादुर पैरा कमांडों के निशाने।
अंधकारों की गहराइयों में, बलिदान की पुकार,
बहादुरी के प्यार में, हर चुनौती के लिए तैयार।

Balidaan: Ode to The Brave Hearts of Rajouri

In the Rajouri hills, where mountains soar,
Five commandos bravely fell to terror's roar.
Their hearts stout, spirits soaring high,
They faced their foes without a sigh.

From shadows deep, cowards struck with dread,
Brave hearts fell, but their legacy won't be shed.
Their sacrifice and valour, shall not disdain,
No mercy for those who bring such pain.

Families mourn, hearts heavy with sorrow,
They won't see their loved ones tomorrow.
Yet, united, we stand, side by side,
In this battle against terror, with growing pride.

Amidst echoes of bravery, together we stand,
A united nation, standing hand in hand.
In the face of darkness, we'll be the light,
For heroes who fought with all their might.

Their sacrifice, a beacon, forever to steer,
In adversity's face, we'll persevere.
With hearts undivided, resolute we'll stand,
Together, we protect our sacred land.

Let our resolve be unwavering and clear,
For our nation's safety, we conquer fear.
With the spirit of heroes, we shall rise,
Stronger and prouder, reaching for the skies.

BRUTAL TRUTH OF WAR

(Image Created by Author)

The brutality of war is only known to a soldier who has been to battle. I have not participated in a conventional war but heard first-hand experiences from my father and met many a war wounded in hospitals post-war. I have been in a counter-terrorism environment and seen its ugly side though. I have also witnessed the scars it leaves a lifetime on the Veer (Brave) Families. Ironically as a nation, we have a short memory of our true heroes and glorify war from the scripts shown on the TV. War makes big news but the fallen soldiers fade with memory. It's a universal truth for all nations. *I have spent many moments of solace in the care of our war-disabled soldiers and the veer families of our fallen soldiers.'* **A soldier's prayer remains – *"Make Peace, Not War."***

"Only the dead have seen the end of war." George Santayana, 1922.

The poem **'Brutal Truths of War',** looks into the bitter reality of war, emphasising the senseless nature of war. It depicts the immense suffering and trauma endured by soldiers and their families. The poem paints a poignant picture of the mayhem and destruction left in the wake of war, with a plea for lasting peace and unity.

"कुछ लक्ष्य इतने योग्य होते हैं कि असफल होना भी गौरवशाली होता है।"
-- कैप्टन मनोज कुमार पांडे - पीवीसी

Brutal Truth of War

In the gory of war, darkness prevails,
A grim reality, where humanity fails.
War does not discern what's just or right,
It chooses who's left to endure the fight.

Young souls thrust into the hellish fray,
Bloodshed and cries, a terrible price to pay.
Politicians scheme in their ivory towers,
Sending them forth in the darkest hours.

War, a tempest with a thunderous roar,
Leaving scars on lands and souls evermore.
Innocent lives lost, children left to mourn,
Families shattered; their spirits forever torn.

A symphony of destruction, a relentless gale,
Cities turned to rubble, an anguished tale,
When the guns fall silent, and the smoke clears,
Victory remains elusive, obscured by lingering fear.

When the hurly-burly's done,
When the battle's lost or won,
War's bitter legacy eternally persists,
Soldiers lost, families in agonising twists.

Let us heed history's harsh call,
May nations never be driven to the wall.
May peace and prosperity define our times,
Humans for Humanity, our sacred chime.

THE FALLEN SOLDIER

(Pic of the author paying homage to Fallen Soldiers at the National War Memorial)

Soldiering is a way of life, not just a profession. It's a life where you proudly sign a blank cheque for your life, payable to the nation. My brother, at the tender age of 20, made the ultimate sacrifice for our country in 1972. Personally, serving in the Kashmir valley from 1996 to 1999, my heart bled many a time having lost many comrades in combat. Yet the most traumatic moment was to be the first to inform the family of a fallen comrade. The memory of which I dread to date and which no words can portray. May God Almighty always bless these brave families and the souls of our **'Fallen Soldiers.'**

This poem '**The Fallen Soldier',** pays tribute to the fallen soldiers who sacrificed their lives for the honour of their nation. It captures the solemnity of their sacrifice and the profound grief experienced by their family. The poem emphasises the duty to honour their brave families and salute those who have given their today for our tomorrow. This evocative epitaph is enshrined on the Kohima war memorial in Nagaland - **'When you go home, tell them of us and say, for your tomorrow we gave our today.'**

ज़माने भर में मिलते हैं आशिक कई,
मगर वतन से ख़ूबसूरत कोई सनम नहीं,
नोटों में लिपटकर, सोने से सिमटकर, मरे हैं कई,
मगर तिरंगे से ख़ूबसूरत कोई क़फ़न नहीं।

The Fallen Soldier

In the hush of night, where shadows dance,
A fallen soldier lies in valour's trance.
He gave his all for a nation's honour and name,
In the darkest hour, he embraced the sombre flame.

Eyes moist, throats choked, hearts in despair,
A nation weeps for its fallen, in silent prayer.
For he, who in battle, stood so tall,
Now answers a higher, celestial call.

In shattered homes, echoes of despair,
The weight of loss, too heavy to bear.
The pain etched deep in each grieving face,
As they long for one more loving embrace.

The flag, now draped in solemn grace,
Bears witness to the hero's final place.
In the hearts of family, forever enshrined,
A sacrifice unmatched, a love undefined.

I am no hero, but I've stood with those who bled,
Felt the family's pain in every tear they shed.
In their darkest hours, I've witnessed their sorrow,
A dreaded dream that knows no bright tomorrow.

So, let us salute the fallen, the brave,
Those they leave behind, our compassion to engrave.
For our tomorrow, they gave their today,
In their sacrifice, we humbly bow and pray.

THE ECHOES OF ELUSIVE PEACE

(Image Source: Yahya Hassouna | AFP | Getty Images)

Wars in the 21st Century are fought to shatter peace. A series of political, social, societal, technological, and ideological storms have shaken the global equilibrium of peace and created instability through war and violence. The policy objectives have transformed from the creation of peace to seeking justice through war. War is inhuman, evil, and destructive. Its destructive character does not differentiate between the enemy and the innocent. War cannot buy justice nor ensure lasting peace. Can we stop this? Can we transform for peace and development?

The poem **'The Echoes of Elusive Peace',** is a call for humans across the globe to unite and put an end to these endless wars.

युद्ध के दिनों में, सूरज उगता नहीं है,
वह हमेशा मनहूस रात होती है।

The Echoes of Elusive Peace

Oh, why can't we find peace in this world to ever last,
Do we wage wars for peace or to shatter peace aghast?
Why can't all brutality and inhuman killings cease,
So, nations and people may unite, and all find peace?

Beneath the shared sky, as brothers and sisters, we stand,
Yet, we battle and destroy, like darkness's cruel hand.
Is it for power, pride, land, ideology or riches to acquire,
That we ignite the world with relentless, destructive fire?

Let's ponder, as we stand on this precipice so high,
Is it worth the countless tears we make others cry?
The echoes of brutality and inhumanity resound,
In our last journey repenting sufferings so profound.

Peace, a beacon of hope, a vision so bright,
A world where all souls reach for the lost light.
No more senseless killings, no more pain or despair,
A planet where all nations unite and lovingly repair.

Let's unite as one, hand in hand, nation by nation,
End the cycle of destruction, and seek a new foundation.
In the garden of humanity, let peace and love bloom,
Banish darkness, let compassion and prosperity consume.

Let the olive branch replace the sword,
Let harmony and prosperity move forward,
Together, we can shape a world just and fair,
Where every soul breathes love's tender air.

ECHOES OF A VANISHING EDEN

(Pic Courtesy undp.org)

The global crisis of environmental degradation looms large, born from the reckless exploitation by mankind of our precious natural resources, unsustainable actions, and unchecked pollution. Its profound, far-reaching consequences adversely affect ecosystems, biodiversity, and human well-being. Deforestation leads to the loss of vital carbon sinks, disrupts habitats, and contributes to adverse climate change. Air, water, or soil pollution poses serious health hazards to the survival of life on earth and in the sea. The concretisation of our world has led to habitat loss, pushing countless species to the brink of extinction. Addressing these crises is an urgent necessity for the survival of our planet and all its inhabitants. But alas will we ever learn!!

This poem, **'Echoes of a Vanishing Eden',** explores the profound changes our world undergoes as human actions reshape the natural environment. It weaves a tapestry of a world where trees, wildlife, and once-thriving ecosystems have been altered or lost. It serves as a lyrical call for action, imploring us to recognise our duty to Earth and to future generations.

पर्यावरण संरक्षण, यही है हमारा धर्म,
यही है हमारा उद्देश्य और कर्म।

Echoes of a Vanishing Eden

I wonder where the trees once stood so grand,
Now felled for furniture by man's own hand.
Beneath layers of cement, green life now hides,
Its vibrant bid for existence slowly subsides.

I ponder where the wildlife now may roam,
In search of new havens, a distant unknown.
Butterflies and sparrows, once a common sight,
No longer flutter and soar in the changing light.

Frogs and toads, where have they withdrawn?
To realms unseen, by humanity's dawn?
Beyond this earthly realm, they may have strayed,
As we sculpt the world, choices are made.

Parks and playgrounds, where have they all gone?
Beneath towering buildings, progress marches on.
The laughter of children, a distant sound,
In a world of concrete, scarcely found.

The freshness of the air, where has it fled?
Drowned in chimneys' smoke, skies turn red.
The mountains, where have they gone?
Replaced by garbage heaps, a vision so wrong.

The world we once knew, can't rewind its chime,
But the choices we make, shape our paradigm.
To save our environment, it's not just a trend,
It's our solemn duty, to Earth and life, let's extend.

CHEERS TO OUR GIRLFRIENDS AND WIVES....
MAY THEY NEVER MEET

(Pic recreated by author)

After completing my school education, I chose a different path, opting for the National Defence Academy (NDA) instead of a traditional college. Our most revered Commandant at NDA was Rear Admiral Manohar Prahlad Awati, PVSM, VrC, a distinguished and transformative figure known for his remarkable sense of humour. On the occasion of Cadets Dinner Night, Admiral Awati would craft delightful toasts that served as a remedy for post-formal event mood swings. One memorable toast he proposed was, **"TO OUR GIRLFRIENDS AND WIVES, ... MAY THEY NEVER MEET."** As cadets under watch, laughter was not permitted even with a serious disposition, yet the toast was raised **"TO THEM"**. This satirical poem is a fond recollection of those unforgettable times when humour and training flourished even in the sternest of circumstances.

'Cheers to our Girlfriends and Wives……May they Never Meet', explores the intricate balance between two contrasting worlds: the steady, loving embrace of committed wives and the exhilarating, unpredictable allure of vivacious girlfriends. With a satirical blend and sentiment, the poem celebrates and humours the unique virtues of both relationships, all while offering a tongue-in-cheek toast to the art of keeping them apart.

हे, खुद ना मिलाना उन्हें, जहन्नुम से बचाना मुझे।
ज़िंदगी की राहों में रास्ते अलग, कहीं ना मिलाना उन्हें।

Cheers to our Girlfriends and Wives......
May they Never Meet

Cheers to our girlfriends and wives, a lively crew,
In separate orbits, with both we rendezvous.
In worlds apart, we dance and prance,
If they converge, sparks ignite, a deadly trance.

Toasting to freedom, with beer and wine,
Girlfriends in rhythm, everything's divine.
Should they meet our wives, what unfolds,
A cosmic clash, a big bang story untold.

To our girlfriends, we say, "Let's hit the town,
With credit cards, let's bring it all down."
But our wives, we vow, "Let's stay serene,
A candlelight dinner, a shared love scene."

At home, tasked to take out the trash,
With girlfriends, we're lightning in a flash.
One says, "Don't stay out too late, my dear,"
The other whispers, "One more honey, Let's cheer!"

To our patient wives, with grace so pure,
To our adventurous girlfriends, love's allure.
We cherish you both in your special way,
But let's keep you apart, night and day.

For if worlds collide, paths intertwine,
We fear the chaos that might define.
So, here's to a toast, with a humorous beat,
Cheers to you both, may you never meet!

AGE IS JUST A FUNNY NUMBER

(Pic recreated by author)

Age, after all, is merely a numerical label, and one only truly ages when one concedes to it. Admittedly, there are certain limitations as one matures, rendering some youthful pursuits less attainable. The joy of being considered the wisest and most well-read is also a characteristic of age. In our WhatsApp group of veterans, we have all the time and all the knowledge to run the world, the nation, and the Defence Forces better. It feels as though our insights possess the potential to alter the course of the grand design. What remains truly uplifting is that our minds continue to function, even if our wisdom occasionally flirts with obsolescence. Yet the fact is that those who dance and play, those who write and speak, and those who paint and sing keep the age away. So, while the body may inevitably age, let the soul remain ever vibrant and youthful.

The poem '***Age is Just a Funny Number'*,** paints a vivid and humorous picture of life as a grand circus. It contrasts the experiences of youth and old age, emphasising the expansion of wisdom and memories even as physical attributes change.

हँसो, मेरे दोस्तों, हर दिन जश्न मनाओ,
जवान मन से, जीवन में खुशियाँ लाओ।

Age is Just a Funny Number

In life's grand circus, we all play a part,
First step to the very last cartwheeling art.
It's a voyage of love, wisdom, and grace,
A dash of humour to light up the place.

When young, our waistlines were trim and fine,
Our minds so expansive, like a grand design.
But as age unfolds, a shift does transpire,
Waistlines expand, broad minds now retire.

We stoop to tie shoelaces and pause with glee,
What else could we do, down on one knee?
In childhood, we yearn for grown-up status,
But in old age, the reverse is the consensus.

With age, belated wisdom, swirling profound,
Time and confidence to run the world around.
Less hair, fewer teeth, and muscles might slack,
Waistlines expand, but confidence stays on track.

Yet friends stick around, a steadfast crew,
Recalling wild tales, naughty quite a few.
Over drinks, with nostalgia fully in sway,
We laugh till we cry, casting age far away.

Let's laugh, my friends, cherish each day,
With minds ever youthful, come what may.
Age is just a number, a playful disguise,
Let go of the ageing machine, be wise.

CELEBRATING LORD KRISHNA'S DIVINE BIRTH

(Image Courtesy – Krishna Radhe Facebook)

Janmashtami, also known as Gokul Ashtami, is a festival celebrated with great fervour and devotion to mark the birth of Lord Krishna. Lord Krishna's birth is believed to have taken place in the city of Mathura in northern India, in a prison cell where his parents, Devaki and Vasudeva, were unjustly imprisoned by Devaki's brother, the wicked King Kansa. It was on this divine night that Lord Krishna made his appearance, escaping Kansa's malevolent grasp. Lord Krishna's divine teachings in the Bhagavad Gita provide profound insights into life's purpose, duty, and the path to spiritual enlightenment.

'Celebrating Lord Krishna's Divine Birth', is a blessing from Lord Krishna, whose path has enriched my life. This poem is a mark of spiritual respect for Lord Krishna. One of the most famous verses from the Bhagavad Gita that speaks of Lord Krishna's divine nature is Chapter 10, Verse 20:

> "*Aham ātmā guḍākeśa*
> *sarva-bhūtāśayasthitaḥ*
> *aham ādiś ca madhyaṁ ca*
> *bhūtānām anta eva ca*"

<u>Translation</u>:

"I am the Self, O Gudakesha, seated in the hearts of all creatures. I am the beginning, the middle, and the end of all beings."

Celebrating Lord Krishna's Divine Birth

In the midnight hour, when stars did gleam,
The world was graced by a divine dream.
On Janmashtami, a sacred morning so rare,
Lord Krishna's divine appearance to prayers.

In Mathura's prison, where shadows did sway,
To King Kansa's dread, on that fateful day.
The eighth avatar of Lord Vishnu, in human form,
Parents Devaki and Vasudeva, divinity to transform.

Yashoda's love, His foster mother's embrace,
Nurtured the Lord with maternal grace.
Little Krishna, mischievous and sublime,
Stole hearts with His flute's sweet rhymes.

With Radha, His beloved, by His side,
In Vrindavan, their love did reside.
Playing the raas with Gopi's, a radiant sight,
Spreading love and joy, both day and night.

As the charioteer of Arjuna, His role was clear,
In the Bhagavad Gita, wisdom He did steer.
A sage and warrior, philosopher and guide,
Lord Krishna's teachings are a blessing to ride.

Essence of Krishna His unwavering exuberance,
In love, in war, His joyful divine countenance.
In His name, may we find our divine grace,
His footsteps, His teachings, in life's space.

LOVE BEYOND DESTINY

(Pic recreated by the author)

In the voyage of life, not every longing and yearning finds its way to fruition. Love and destiny intertwine, their courses sometimes merging and at other times, drifting apart as the tides of time ebb and flow. At various points, every individual has experienced a crush or harboured a secret fantasy. I, too, have been ensnared by such emotions.

'Love Beyond Destiny', encapsulates a fictional love story that narrates the poignant tale of two souls bound together by a profound connection, only to be torn apart by the cruel hands of destiny and the vast chasm of distance that separates them. The poem explores themes of love, loss, hope, and resilience, with a touch of mysticism as it hints at a reunion in the afterlife.

मोहब्बत दो दिलों की दास्तान है,
हर तन्हाई का नया इम्तिहान है,
कुदरत ने दीवार बनाई, पर मंज़िल हमारी एक है।

Love Beyond Destiny

Whispering willows, flowering bloom, enchanting spring,
Heavens smiled, our gaze met, love's melodies to sing.
Beneath the romantic sky, we took a lover's flight that day,
A blissful journey cast, love beyond destiny there to stay.

We danced, our hearts entwined in ecstasy's sweet grace,
Time held no dominion, nights in passion's embrace.
Intense and emotional, a bonding full of caring,
It bloomed and blossomed with life's sharing.

A thread of the past, an invisible bond steadfast,
Promises of reincarnation, dreaming it would last.
But then came the storm, blinding and splitting our way,
It was not us, but cruel destiny that washed us away.

Decades apart, yet something invisible defied sanity,
We knew it was a fantasy but never accepted the reality.
Our worlds too distant to retrieve what was gone,
A realm of love, hope, and joy, once brightly drawn.

You became the healer and I the mask of pretense,
You sang the songs, and I basked in love essence.
Every love has its smiles, every dream its bend,
Ours followed the script, reaching its inevitable end.

Life moves on, memories linger in the air,
A part of you forever in my soul there.
Sunrise to sunset, I silently watch the hues fade,
Rekindling our memories through light and shade.

BOUNDLESS LOVE: A SYMPHONY OF SOULFUL HEARTS

(Pic recreated by the author)

In the journey of life, few emotions possess the extraordinary ability to transcend the confines of time and space as profoundly as love. Love is a potent force that kindles the depths of the soul, serves as a guiding light through the labyrinthine journey of existence, and adorns our world with vibrant hues of passion, patience, respect, understanding, and profound connection. Yet, it is not confined to mere visual allure; instead, it delves deeper into the realms of the soul, emphasising the significance of respect and mutual understanding over fleeting physical pleasures. As a man who leads with his heart, love has been the most unifying force in my journey, transcending the boundaries of the mind and binding me to the essence of the soul.

'Boundless Love: A Symphony of Soulful Hearts', is a poetic exploration of the profound journey that love takes us on. In this poetic voyage, we delve into the realms of passion, honesty, respect, and patience, celebrating the resilience of love's flame even in the face of life's storms. Let our hearts dance in harmony, and the melody of love will resonate eternally.

मोहब्बत वही कर सकता है जो इज़्ज़त का हकदार हो,
इज़्ज़त वही कर सकता है जिसकी मोहब्बत बरकरार हो।

Boundless Love: A Symphony of Soulful Hearts

In passion's realm where hearts ignite,
Love's flame burns fierce, a guiding light.
Through honesty, our souls entwine,
In truth's embrace, love's stars align.

Respect blooms like a fragrant flower,
Embracing flaws, nurturing each hour.
In the garden of our love's embrace,
Cherished moments find their sacred place.

Patience paints our canvas with delight,
A masterpiece of day and tranquil night.
With fortitude, we seize the day's array,
Hand in hand, through life's uncharted way.

In laughter's grace and shared tears, we bear,
This bond of love, so extraordinary, and rare.
It's a melody, a dance, an endless song,
A love that's pure, where we truly belong.

Through stormy seas and skies of endless blue,
This love endures, forever tried and true.
A beacon in the darkest, loneliest night,
Guiding us with its unwavering light.

So let love's symphony resound and sway,
With honesty, truth, and respect day by day.
In patience's grace and fiery, ardent embrace,
Our souls dance freely, boundless in space.

MAKING MEMORIES, NOT DREAMS

(Pic by the Author)

Way back in school, reading Shakespeare, I vividly recollect an enlightening verse composed on the names of his books:

> *"Life is a Tempest,*
> *Not a Mid-Summer Night's Dream,*
> *But it is a Comedy of Errors,*
> *So, Spend It as You Like It."*

The last line touched a chord that we need to add life to our years and not just years to our lives. Age is just another crazy number, and staying young is optional. The quest to traverse life's journey till the end with no regrets or missing desires thus must become a beacon of life. So, friends, make your dreams come true and your memories beautiful. *'Life is short, time is fast, and there are no replays or rewinds'* so just enjoy every moment and add more life to each moment.

'Making Memories, Not Dreams', explores the heart of human existence and weaves a narrative of life's journey, emphasising the importance of cherishing memories over ephemeral dreams. It celebrates the dance of time and the intrinsic value of recollection as a means of feeling truly alive. Ultimately, the message is to leave this world with memories and not dreams.

ज़िंदगी के इस सफर में,
यादों को पलकों में छुपा लो।
ज़िंदगी के हर लम्हे को,
खुशियों का नया सफर बना लो।

Making Memories, Not Dreams

In the canvas of life, colours softly blend,
New adventures, memories at each bend.
As seasons gracefully dance, years swiftly pass,
Each memory's a gem, through the looking glass.

In the fleeting hours, beneath the endless skies,
Recollecting each moment, of our existence's rise.
For the goal is clear, as the river's flow,
To die with memories, not dreams aglow.

Dawn's tender embrace and the twilight's kiss,
We'll find life's magic, an eternal bliss.
With each step taken, each mountain climbed,
We amass memories, treasures of our time.

Not mere idle wishes or whimsical schemes,
But memories woven into the tapestry of dreams.
Laughter, tears, moments of grace,
Find a home in our love's warm embrace.

When the time of farewell inevitably draws near,
Our memories will linger, soothing every fear.
In the end, it's not dreams that truly define,
But the memories we craft, a life so sublime.

So, strive to live, embrace each day's grace,
Let memories bloom, in life's tender embrace.
Seize the moments, hold memories clear,
Let laughter and love make your journey dear.

ODE TO THE NOBLE STEEDS

(Pic: Authors Maternal Grandfather. Maj Harbans Rai of Martand Lancer, Military Secretary, during a review of Parade by HH Maharaja of Rewa State)

Horses, often referred to as noble steeds, have held a special place in human history and culture for centuries. Their grace in motion, flowing manes, and powerful stature make them not only loyal companions but also symbols of beauty and nobility.

As a young kid, I learned horse riding in the Army Cantonment. At NDA, I joined the Riding Club, though never graduated to be an elite rider. On commissioning, we wore our winter mess cavalry dress – blue patrol with breeches and wellingtons with spurs. The romanticism for horses only grew through the ages.

'Ode to the Noble Steeds', captures the essence of horses as majestic beings, celebrating their grace, strength, and unwavering loyalty. The poem paints a vivid portrait of these noble animals, emphasising their historical significance in various roles, from workhorses to fiery steads in battle. The poem pays tribute to these magnificent steeds, highlighting their integral place in the tapestry of our shared heritage.

जंग के तूफान में, घोड़े हैं शूरवीर की पहचान,
हर जीत में उनका है बलिदान महान।

Ode to The Noble Steeds

Majestic steeds, wild and free,
Running through fields as far as can see.
Graceful movements, strong and sound,
Their beauty and grace, a sight so profound.

Manes and tails, flowing in the breeze,
As they gallop through the open trees.
Hooves pounding on the earth below,
Their power and strength on full show.

From the humble workhorse to the fiery steed,
Each one's a marvel, born of noble breed.
Their loyalty and spirit, so pure and true,
They give their all in everything they do.

In times of war, they charged ahead,
Their courage and valour, forever widespread.
Their unwavering strength, an ally in strife,
Their bond with riders, the essence of life.

Oh, noble steeds, your spirit untamed,
In the annals of time, your legend is framed.
In the tapestry of time, your hoofprints remain,
A testament to strength, through joy and pain.

So let us remember these noble steads,
Their beauty, power, and grace never cease.
Without them, our history would not be the same,
More than mere animals, they're part of our fame.

ENCHANTING HAZEL EYES

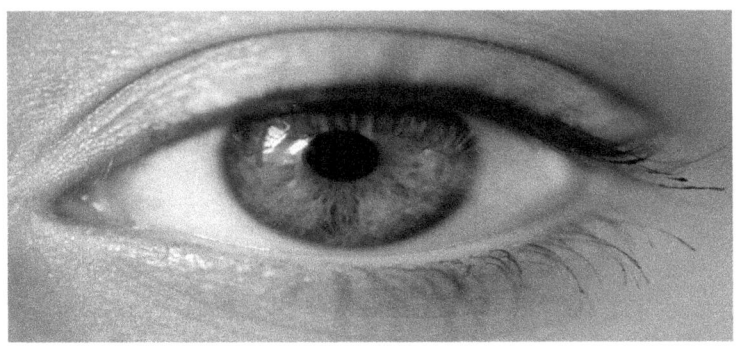

(Pic courtesy Pinterest)

Life is a romantic journey where eyes meet and hearts beat, yet the words remain elusive. It's just that momentary gaze that spreads a smile, which says it all. Possibly the most expressive and beautiful part of the human body are the eyes, which can never lie. They have a direct lightning connection with the heart before the brain. The third eye (inner eye) is a mystical invisible eye, usually depicted as located on the forehead, which provides perception beyond ordinary sight. Such is the deep impact of enchanting eyes, which leave a lifetime memory.

Hazel eyes are captivating and unique, often characterised by a blend of brown, green, and sometimes even hints of blue. They are often described as having a mysterious and enchanting trance. One look, and they are sure to hypnotise you. I, too, had my moment, lost in the allure of hazel eyes. *"Some eyes touch you more than hands ever could."*

'Enchanting Hazel Eyes', explores the profound and enchanting looks of hazel eyes, weaving a tapestry of emotions, passion, and longing. The verses romantically describe the enchanting eyes, portraying them with emotion and love. The poem conveys the enduring power of hazel eyes to stir the soul and kindle the flames of love, even when distant.

हिरणी सी ये आँखें, कुछ बातें कह जाती हैं,
कुदरत की देन, ये हमें प्यार में डूबा जाती हैं।

Enchanting Hazel Eyes

Hazel eyes that gleam with love,
A sight of pure passion so rare.
As if the heavens up above,
Have crafted them with care.

The way they light up with delight,
Or simmer with emotion deep.
It's like they hold the stars at night,
Many a romantic secret to keep.

In them, I see a world of wonder,
A world that's soft and bright.
A world that's filled with thunder,
Yet calm as a summer's night.

Oh, hazel eyes, how they enchant,
With every glance and gaze.
They stir the soul, they make us pant,
In a lover's warm embrace.

With eyes like these, love knows no end,
A flame that burns so bright.
A passion that cannot bend,
In the arms of sweet delight.

And as time goes on, I still yearn,
For those hazel eyes, a cherished sight.
Though distance keeps us apart, I discern,
Their memories bring back heartfelt delight.

SOMEONE…. SOMEWHERE…. SOMEDAY

(Pic recreated by the author)

In the journey of life, there is always someone…. somewhere…. someday by your side to see you brave the storms of life. This is called *'Sharing and Caring'*, the essence of life through the many storms. I have always been taught a phrase: *'So shall it also pass'*, meaning no storms are permanent and *'when the going gets tough, the tough get going'*. For all of us life has its ups and downs for someone…. somewhere…someday, so be that pillar of strength for them to tide over the wave. When I was young, it was my family by my side and after marriage, it was me by their side. In the Army, which remains the most stressful and high-risk way of life, the band of brothers, be it in combat or peacetime, are there with you always, everywhere, and every time.

Resilience is their strength, and camaraderie is their signature.

'Someone.... Somewhere.... Someday', is a lyrical poem that invites us on a journey through life's challenges and triumphs. Amidst the stars and moonlit paths, the poem weaves a tapestry of hope and resilience. It inspires us to find strength in the face of adversity and to embrace the symphony of life's experiences. The poem delves into the beauty of life's journey and the power of the human spirit.

दिल के दामन में छुपे हैं वो, कोई हमें उनसे अब मिला दे,
'कहीं कोई, किसी दिन, किसी जगह' हमको अपना हमसफर बना ले।

Someone.... Somewhere.... Someday

When shadows fall and courage wanes,
Lean on me through life's storms and rains.
I'll be your friend, a steadfast guide,
In every storm, I'll stand beside.

I'll help you carry burdens, heavy and long,
Together, we'll find the strength to be strong.
For in this journey, we're never alone,
Lean on me, my friend; our love has grown.

When tears like raindrops start to fall,
And darkness seems to conquer all.
Look up above, find solace there,
Moonlit path to guide you somewhere.

The symphony of laughter and pain,
The threads of joy and tears like rain.
They shape the tapestry of your soul,
A masterpiece that makes you whole.

So let the winds of passion soar,
And let your spirit freely explore.
For in your heart, the fire burns,
Let the symphony of life return.

And, before we journey into the night,
Let us open our hearts to the starlight.
For in the vastness of the cosmic chime,
Lies 'Someone...Somewhere...Someday' divine.

EMBERS OF CANDLELIGHT

(Image Courtesy: Lifestyle Asia)

In the subtle dance of light and shadow, we find a metaphor for the profound connections we share in life. Just as the flame of a candle and its glow coexist, our relationships, too, intertwine to create something beautiful and enduring. The flame symbolises love, warmth, and resilience, qualities that sustain us through life's trials and tribulations. Yet it selflessly melts away for others' light. As we hold close to these connections, let us remember the power of love, sacrifice, and the warmth of human bonds. Like the candle, we may eventually melt away, but the light and memories we leave behind continue to illuminate the hearts of those we touch. So, cherish every moment, every flicker, and every embrace, for in these simple gestures, we discover the profound beauty of life's essence. Let the candle be our light.

'Embers of Candlelight', delves into the symbolism of a candle's light, depicting it as a guardian of inner light, a source of solace, and a soothing presence during life's darkest hours. The verses emphasise the power of this bond, where two spirits intertwine like dancing shadows, creating a magnificent tapestry of love.

मोमबत्ती की रौशनी जैसा दिल का प्यार,
रात के अंधेरे में बनाती है दिलदार।

Embers of Candlelight

I am the flicker in your heart's embrace,
I am the glow that lights up your space.
I am the warmth on a cold winter's night,
I am the guardian of your inner light.

You find solace in my gentle glow,
In your sanctuary, I softly bestow.
You trust me to brighten your darkest hour,
In your haven, I hold a soothing power.

Hold me close, let our spirits entwine,
In this dance of shadows, your light defines.
Together, we create a tapestry so grand,
In this bond, forever we'll stand.

In the stillness of the night, we find our way,
Guided by the flicker, in the dark, we'll stay.
With every heartbeat, our love does bloom,
In the dance of shadows, there's no gloom.

As you seek refuge in my gentle flame,
In the garden of love, we both lay claim.
Hold me close, let our souls' interplay,
Till we melt into dawn's first ray.

So, stand by me, as we journey on,
In the love's flame, our fears gone.
Each passing moment, our bond grows,
In the soft, warm glow, our spirits flow.

THOSE WERE THE DAYS MY FRIEND

(Pic of the author with friends - School Days)

Life is a romantic journey for all, some said... some unsaid. Yet it's friends and their memories that make the journey memorable with an evergreen smile. Youth have a special place in this bonding, with jumping hearts, little responsibility, and plenty of innocence. So was my journey full of fun and friends who endeared themselves to a lifetime friendship to cherish. That bunking of classes, those picnics, those messages concealed in books, those movies, and those jam sessions still bring about an adrenaline rush and a blush on the wrinkled face. Memories vivid, hearts young, though decades have gone by.

The poem *'Those Were the Days, My Friend',* fondly reminisces about the cherished friendships that enriched the poet's life. The verses capture the essence of enduring bonds, shared laughter, and the warmth of true friendship. Through sparkling imagery and expressive language, the poem celebrates the value of these connections and the enduring memories they have created.

यह मोहब्बत का शहर है जनाब, यहां सवेरा सूरज से नहीं, किसी दिलदार की धड़कन से होता है।

Those Were the Days My Friend

My friends who've stolen my heart's embrace,
With a charm that time could never erase.
Capturing my soul, their beauty and grace,
In my heart, they've found a forever place.

Each one of you, a unique bond we've shared,
Love and friendship, how deeply we've cared.
You've brought joy and laughter, moments rare,
Through life's challenges, together we've fared.

With sparkling eyes and smiles, infectious and true,
You've brightened my world as the seasons flew.
Your kindness and warmth, like morning dew,
In the treasure trove of friendships, you're my crew.

Every connection with you, a story we've etched,
Friendship's embrace, in every storm, we've fetched.
Though paths may diverge, our hearts remain aligned,
In life's grand narrative, your presence forever defined.

Life's journey with you, a grand and vibrant stage,
Sweet memories cherished, no matter the age.
May your days be filled with love, joy at each stage,
Blessings aplenty, gratitude on life's each page.

As time gracefully dances on, let's joyfully toast,
To the memories where laughter mattered most.
Though miles may separate, our bonds never lost,
In sweet remembrance, our friendship uppermost.

THE RAY OF HOPE

(Image Courtesy Daily Excelsior)

In an Army life, where challenges and turbulence are plentiful, *'hope of success rather than fear of failure'* guides the journey. As someone who enjoys backronyms, HOPE stands for **'Hang On Pain Ends.'** Hope is also a desire to be fulfilled. I had a desire to become a Tankman and hoped to be one in every dream. Some dreams and hopes, with perseverance, come true. Many times, in my life, adversity and challenges beyond expectations have emerged. Yet the silent prayers and positive thoughts have swayed with time to let those moments pass and open the doors of better times. Hope is both a blissful destination and a remedy for grief.

'The Ray of Hope', is an inspirational poetic odyssey about the power of positivity and hope in the face of life's challenges and adversities. Hope serves as an unyielding anchor in troubled waters and a source of resolute courage in challenging times. It tells us that hope is not just a fleeting emotion but a ray of heavenly glow that brightens our path, no matter the adversity.

कभी ख़ुशी की आशा,
कभी गम की निराशा,
सपनों का साथी, है यह ख़्वाब,
बस आशा के साथ, आगे बढ़ते रहना, जनाब।

The Ray of Hope

In life's tempestuous sea, we sail our course,
Seeking anchors, fragile as a whisper, of course.
In troubled waters, we grope and we cope,
What truly sustains us is the lifeline of hope.

From innocent children, dreams unbound,
To souls in the twilight, stories to astound,
In every heart, in every dream's scope,
The ray of light, our unbreakable hope.

It's the calm in chaos, taking fearless flight,
A flicker in the darkest, a beacon in the night,
Courage to keep faith when shadows encroach,
Through trials by fire, it's what we'll approach.

In desperate hours, when life's traffic is a maze,
Hope, defying logic, in the heart's secret phase,
Hangs by the thread of dreams yet untold,
Guiding us to futures where promises unfold.

Believe in yourself, with hope as your guide,
Let it sweep away fears, let your spirit glide,
For hope mends your soul, without cease,
Leading you to a tranquil, eternal peace.

So, hope for the best, let your heart take flight,
In the darkest hour, it'll be your guiding light,
With hope as your compass, forever in your soul,
You'll find eternal solace, and blessings forever roll.

WHEN COMPASSION ECHOES

(Pic of the Author in Bali)

Life in my younger years was much simpler and more bonded both to humanity and nature. I remember our bonding with neighbours as an extended family and holidays with relatives being so much fun. The expectations were none, the joys simple, and the bonding strong. We had real friends, not virtual friends, and played real games rather than virtual games. We were closer to the real world than to the charm of the virtual world. Have we transitioned from a world of compassion, love, and spreading happiness to a selfish world of extracting the most for our own benefit? From a world of tolerance and harmony to one of hatred and disdain? As I traverse my journey, these questions continue to haunt me.

'When Compassion Echoes', is an emotive poetic joint composition by a budding poetess, **Amulya Anil** and me, that explores the yearning for a world once filled with goodness and compassion, now seemingly lost amid discord and dislike. The poem reflects on the passage of time and the desire to rediscover the values of empathy and unity. The poem invites readers to embark on a journey of rekindling kindness and nurturing the seeds of humanity in an increasingly selfish and divisive world.

कहाँ गए वो बचपन के सुनहरे दिन,
यारों की यारी, खुशियों से भरे दिन।
क्यों हो गये हम इतने अनजान,
ला दो वापस वो सुनहरे पल जो थी हमारी पहचान।

When Compassion Echoes

I hope secretly, to find that place
Where all the goodness had vanished,
And venture again into the space,
Where a kind heart once perished.

The clock kept ticking,
And I kept wondering,
What happened to all the love the world once knew?
Why is dislike the mandate of the new?

In the world that is amiss,
I hope to find, all that was lost,
The love and the goodness,
The kind heart, the most.

In the depths of searching, I yearn to uncover
The echoes of compassion, long buried and concealed,
For in this realm of chaos, where shadows hover,
I seek the light of empathy to be revealed.

Amidst the clamour of hatred and disdain,
I dream of harmony, where differences unite,
In that place, where whispers of kindness bloom,
I'll gather the fragments, like petals on the wind.

Oh, let me traverse this path of rediscovery,
Where love's symphony resonates in every hue,
For in nurturing the seeds of humanity,
We'll rebuild a world where kindness shines anew.

EMBRACE THE JOY OF SMILE

(Pic: Author Generated)

Smile has a universal language and an infectious reflection. A leader often leads his team with trust and confidence reflected in his smile. Such is a soldier's journey where, even under adversity, the power of a smile can add calmness in a storm. Smiling even at a glance is a silent expression of love and happiness, enough to stir the heart and soul. Such is the power of a simple, innocent smile.

My poem **'Embrace the Joy of Smile',** celebrates the joy of a smile to bring happiness to our journey of life. In a busy, rushed, modern world, a single smile can create ripples of positivity, uniting love and spreading joy universally. My verses remind us to smile more often, love more deeply, and create a world of happiness.

"तबस्सुम जब तक है। उम्मीद है के दुनिया कायम है।"
------ *गुलज़ार*

Embrace the Joy of Smile

In a world where time swiftly flows,
Uncertain paths, where life often sways,
Choose your companions with wisdom each day,
Life's too short to squander in disarray.

Life is a treasure trove, let's unwrap with glee,
Embrace those who set your heart dancing free,
Their laughter and love, pure happiness,
In their presence, lives filled with tenderness.

Like sunbeams, they warm the coldest days,
In a world of wonder, love's sweet refrain plays,
A smile, a ripple, spreading far and wide,
One smile ignites thousands, side by side.

A treasure so pure, for love is the key,
In a universal chorus, joy's melody,
A smile's ripple, spreading far and wide,
Bringing hearts together side by side.

It costs us nothing, yet grants us it all,
A seraphic smile, a love that won't fall.
In this world, where anger and hate may strive,
With a smile, let's spread happiness and revive.

So, let your smile bloom, let love take its flight,
In spreading joy and laughter, our guiding light,
In a world where kindness, like a river, flows,
Let's smile and love, where happiness grows.

GOLF: A LIFE'S ECSTASY

(Pic of the Author at a Golf)

The **'Golf Bug'** bit me late in life. I always thought golf was only a lazy game for the retired. Yet when handed over the patronship of the course in Jodhpur on taking over a Brigade, I had no choice but to buy a golf set and venture into unknown vistas. Soon the bug bit me for life, and I became a golf lover by design. Post retirement, with both the time and the need to be away from the house, golf kept me physically and mentally active. Golf is also a great leveller of life and a game of gentlemen with subtle humour.

"Give me golf clubs, fresh air, and a beautiful partner, and you can keep the clubs and the fresh air."

– **Jack Benny.**

'Golf: A Life's Ecstasy', is a poetic exploration of the connection between golf and life's journey. It highlights with humour the challenges and surprises golfers face, symbolised by sand traps and water hazards, and underscores the importance of maintaining composure and having fun. Golf is a mirror reflecting the ebbs and flows of life, imparting valuable lessons along the way.

गोल्फ के खेल में रंग है और स्वाद,
हर दर्द को भुलाकर वहाँ बसता है प्यार।

Golf: A Life's Ecstasy

The love of golf, a boundless passion,
A game of patience and action.
A journey filled with highs and lows,
But always worth the joy it bestows.

The gentle breeze, the green scenic sight,
A moment of serenity, a peaceful delight.
The course, a haven, a tranquil therapy,
Where time takes a bow, life's ecstasy.

With every shot, confidence swells,
But then it hits the trees as well.
Life surprises you and questions your form,
But we move on, no option but to be calm.

The sand traps, the water hazards, get us slow,
As the ball lands in them with unbelievable flow.
But we keep playing with a smile on our faces,
Knowing that we are not here to win any races.

And then there's the putt, the bane of the game,
Where the ball rolls along lighting the flame.
Aiming for the cup with all precision and insight,
But it rolls away like a mischievous sprite.

Golf is a game more than just the score,
It's a game to have fun, nothing more.
A mirror to our blissful journey's ebb and flow,
Teaching us lessons as we swing and grow.

HUMANS FOR HUMANITY

(Image Courtesy: Indian Army 'Sarv Dharam Sthal' Udchalo.com)

'The Idea of India' is a phrase that is a tapestry woven from the threads of unity in diversity, secularism, inclusivity and tolerance, democratic governance, cultural heritage, social justice, and economic progress. It is the true identity of Bharat, in the spirit of *'Nation Above All'*. It is also reflected in the national anthem and the souls of most Indians. The most apt symbol of secular outlook and nationalism is the Indian Armed Forces. They believe in *'Sarv Dharam Stal'* (all religions in one place) as a place of worship irrespective of caste, creed, or religion. They go to war shoulder-to-shoulder for the nation. Indian culture and heritage are reflected in the Sanskrit phrase *'Vasudhaiva Kutumbakam'* which means 'the world is

one family'. It is a philosophical concept that embodies the idea of universal brotherhood and the interconnectedness of all beings.

The poem '**Humans for Humanity'**, extols unity among the diverse voices, faiths, and backgrounds that enrich our world, emphasising that love is the universal truth that binds us all. The poem calls for humanity to heed God's timeless lesson of love, peace, and harmony.

"मुझे वह धर्म पसंद है जो स्वतंत्रता, समानता और बंधुत्व सिखाता है।"
……. Dr B R Ambedkar

Humans for Humanity

In the universe woven by God's hand,
Emerged Humans, a masterpiece so grand.
Hearts beating as one, souls united at birth,
Yet diverging paths we journeyed on Mother Earth.

God made humans, in His image, divine,
But borders emerged, divisive, malign.
Caste, colour and creed, they wove,
Hatred above humanity they drove.

Let's weave a tapestry of mutual respect,
Reflect on each teaching, to introspect.
Love, our common thread, let's share,
In life's tapestry, spread harmony and care.

Unity's symphony, a melody so grand,
Different voices entwined, every land.
Backgrounds diverse, faiths intertwine,
Humans for humanity soulful and divine.

Religious places, sacred shrines aglow,
Symbols radiant, where spirits flow.
Windows to the divine, varied and true,
One truth prevails, love's eternal cue.

Remember, as we journey along,
God's unity message, love ever strong.
Guided by harmony, peace is our goal,
Unity's flame must illuminate each soul.

JOURNEY OF CONNECTION: THE BRIDGE OF LIFE

(Pic generated by the author)

In life, both destiny and people help you to cross obstacles by being the blissful bridge, in my youth, it was my parents whose guidance and encouragement made every adversity look small. As I grew and joined the army, it was my colleagues and fellow soldiers, and we as a team could achieve what possibly individually was not possible. The support system within the Army as an extended family remains unsurpassable in uniform or even after it. I owe my success and all awards to the men I commanded and the superiors I was blessed to serve, who remained the bridge in my life's journey. I hope I did become one too for others.

The poem **_Journey of Connection: The Bridge of Life_**, highlights life's journey as a bridge connecting paths and emphasises the importance of offering help and support to others in times of need. It acknowledges the resilience we develop through facing trials and urges us to extend a helping hand without favour or fear. Prioritising love, cherishing connections, and expressing gratitude for simple joys enrich our lives.

जीवन के सफर में निकले थे हम अकेले,
तकदीर ने लिए बेहिसाब इंतेहान सबसे पहले,
लोग मिलते गए हर मोड़ पर और कारवां बनता गया,
जीवन की हर मुश्किल पार करने का एक सहारा मिलता गया।

Journey of Connection: The Bridge of Life

In life's journey, at times we're led,
To be a bridge where paths are spread.
Across troubled waters, we stride with grace,
A helping hand appears, a guiding embrace.

Rough seas may churn, and days be scary,
But strength within, we need not bury.
We've all faced trials, torn by storms apart,
Yet emerged resilient, with a mended heart.

Grasp the hand that's offered near,
Extend your own without favour or fear.
For life's tapestry is woven strong,
Intertwined hearts, where we belong.

Cherish those close, before they depart,
Heal the wounds that divide the heart.
Prioritise love over triviality,
Share and care with pure sincerity.

For life's made rich by simple joys,
Love's embrace, and laughter's noise.
Express gratitude for every touch,
Every little thing means so much.

So heed this tale, let your heart sing,
With the power of connection, let it ring.
In this symphony, together we're caught,
Finding strength and love, as we're taught.

SENTINELS OF MOTHER EARTH

(Pic: Author at a Tree Plantation Drive)

Over the span of more than six decades, I've observed the once lush earth transform into a barren landscape. I've watched as the air's freshness and purity have given way to a toxic haze. Be it in uniform or as a civilian, I've made efforts to contribute to environmental protection and raise awareness amongst the people. My friends, family and I share a deep love for plants and greenery, yet we've witnessed trees being felled and hills flattened to make way for highways and housing developments. There was little we could do besides raise our voices and express our concerns. It leaves me pondering the environment that our future generations will inherit amidst the ongoing climate change and environmental degradation crisis.

This poem, **'Sentinels of Mother Earth',** portrays the lament of a world in distress due to human actions, symbolised by fading breezes and marred landscapes. It captures the poignant decline of nature, from desolate forests to polluted rivers, and the encroachment of plastic in the oceans. The poem also inspires hope and unity, urging us to protect and preserve the environment, reduce waste, nurture biodiversity, and harness renewable energy.

पर्यावरण की सुरक्षा में हमारी खुशहाली,
प्राकृतिक सौंदर्य को बचाने से जीवन मधुशाली।

Sentinels of Mother Earth

Amidst the whispers of fading breeze,
World once vibrant begins to wheeze.
Nature's masterpiece marred by heedless hands,
Environment degradation scars Earth's land.

Forests, once lush, now stand in mournful gloom,
Their ancient echoes silenced; their spirits consumed.
Rivers weep tears, skies bear disarray,
Mountains erode, as nature fades away.

Oceans, scenic with life's wondrous array,
Now grapple beneath plastic's relentless display.
Creatures falter, their homes in decline,
Humanity's greed is a relentless malignity.

Let's unite, hand in hand, for our sacred land,
Protect and preserve, in a pledge we stand.
To reduce waste, let pollution wane,
Embrace sustainable choices, in Nature's name.

Harness the winds, the sun's brilliant light,
Embrace renewable energy, banish the night.
Plant trees, nurture life's rich diversity,
Revive a world of ecological unity.

Let us unite, for a renewed Earth's birth right,
Defend and protect with all our might.
Hand in hand, protect the environment, be brave,
Resilient earth, our home, our mission to save.

SPIRITUAL JOURNEY: AWAKENING OF THE SOUL

(Image Courtesy: Why Hindu.com)

Amid the challenges brought by COVID-19, I embarked on a transformative journey from a professional soldier to a spiritual seeker. Online Vedanta classes and Atmabodha, for which I am indebted to a spiritual soul, **Dr Nidhi Umang Budhraja,** who awakened my soul and sparked this evolution in me. She is a multi-talented and multifaceted role model woman of substance. I delved into the teachings of the Bhagavad Gita, initiated meditation, and found solace in spirituality. This period led to self-realisation, with the profound verse **'Sath Cit Ananda'**, a reality seen through the discovery of Brahman as *'Sath'* or ultimate being, *'cit'* or pure consciousness, and *'ananda'* or perfect bliss.

'Spiritual Journey: Awakening of the Soul', delves into the profound realm of spirituality and the inner awakening of the soul. The poem portrays the soul as a mystic beacon, transcending earthly limitations to embrace a higher spiritual reality. It conveys the idea of a transformative awakening, where the soul's connection with truth is unveiled, leading to joy and harmony.

One of the most celebrated and often quoted verses is from the Rigveda (1.164.20), and it is known as the **"Gayatri Mantra."** This verse is a hymn to the Sun God and is revered for its spiritual and philosophical significance.

ॐ भूर्भुवः स्वः
तत्सवितुर्वरेण्यं
भर्गो देवस्य धीमहि
धियो यो नः प्रचोदयात्।

Spiritual Journey: Awakening of the Soul

Beyond what mortal eyes behold,
Truth resides, many stories untold.
Soul, a mystic beacon burning bright,
Unveils the path through spiritual light.

Numbed are the senses, earthly bound,
Soul ascends, where echoes resound.
Past veils of illusion, woven and spun,
To reality's realm, where truth is one.

Bound by flesh and bones, body journeys on,
Soul, a cosmic traveller, strong and drawn.
Deep in its core, a sacred fire resides,
Guiding wisdom where divinity hides.

Material world, a tapestry of form,
The spiritual world, beyond the storm.
Mirror reflecting what's pure and true,
Worlds unveiled, vivid in the soul's view.

Awakening, a sunrise within the heart,
Petals unfurl, embracing each part.
Transcendent joy in the spiritual art,
Limitations fade, and new life starts.

Within, seek the union of soul and truth,
Let your spirit shine, a radiant sleuth.
Eyes that perceive beyond finite lands,
Symphony of hope at Almighty's hands.

SWAY IN THE RHYTHM OF LIFE

(Image Courtesy: pexels.com/search/sunrise)

Life is a journey filled with a multitude of experiences, each moment a unique note in its grand symphony. It encompasses a bundle of emotions, relationships, challenges, and joys. It also has its share of sorrow and tears. It has its tense moments and stress. Yet after each dark cloud, is a ray of sunshine. Mine was no different. Many nights I danced all night, and many times I tossed and turned in sleepless nights. From the challenges of existence to the profound connections we forge, life is a journey of growth, discovery, and self-realisation. Life is a lesson taught one day and a joy celebrated the next day. Ultimately, life's beauty lies in its unpredictability and sway. My favourite self-talk:

"One day your entire life will flash in front of you. Make sure it's worth watching."

'Sway in the Rhythm of Life', is a poetic journey that invites readers to immerse themselves in the intricate melodies of existence. This poem weaves together themes of hope, love, compassion, and mindfulness, encouraging us to embrace the present moment. It celebrates the profound connections between our breaths and the tapestry of time, emphasising the importance of nurturing our well-being and aligning heart and soul. The poem encourages us to embrace the freedom of the present and allow the enduring power of love to guide us through the future.

जीवन का सफर, एक अनमोल दास्तान,
हर मोड़ पर नई राहें, नया गुलिस्तां।

Sway in the Rhythm of Life

In the rhythm of life, melodies softly play,
Hope, love, and joy in each harmonious sway.
Inhale the essence, let it fill your soul,
Exhale the kindness, let compassion console.

With every breath, a beacon, a rhyme,
Illuminating paths through the tapestry of time.
Life's intricate threads to the divine whole,
Nurture your well-being, align heart and soul.

Infuse your moments with vivacious grace,
Celebrate the present, in its warm embrace.
Every moment is a gift to cherish,
Embrace, the joy of life to flourish.

Wisdom wears disguises, humble yet profound,
In failures and heartaches, treasures are found.
From hardships, emerges a resilient sway,
Moulding and shaping us along the way.

Release regrets, leave worries behind,
Embrace the present, freedom you'll find.
In the rhythm of life, a fleeting trance,
Sway in abandonment, this cosmic dance.

For life's a journey, ever-changing, vast,
In its grand tapestry, we're all cast.
With each moment, let love steadfast,
Sway in the rhythm of life, till the very last.

SWEET SURRENDER

(Pic Courtesy: Productive Flourishing)

Surrender for a military man – NEVER; but Surrender to Life's joy – FOREVER. One has so often in life heard the phrase 'Let Go' or 'Detachment'. Yet as I grew, I learned better words for the reality of life: **'Blissipline'** (Blissfulness + Discipline) and **'Detached Attachment'**. *'Blissipline'* is the art of wholeheartedly committing to a goal while relishing every step of the journey, seeing the future, and letting go of the past. *'Detached Attachment'* is when you let go of control and allow your possessions to come and go. In life, you are not the owner, but the caretaker. Love it when it belongs to you, and sweet surrender when it's time for it to go. This is the harsh reality of life which will give you Blissipline.

'Sweet Surrender', is an inspirational poem that delves into the profound wisdom of embracing life's challenges and uncertainties with grace. Through verses, it highlights the transformative power of surrender, emphasising that it is not a sign of defeat but rather a path to authenticity and inner strength. The poem encourages us to release the inner battles, allowing life to take its natural course and revealing the hidden reservoirs of resilience within. It speaks of the inevitability of hardships but also the promise of brighter days ahead, where the colours of life's tapestry re-emerge after the storm. "Sweet Surrender" celebrates the beauty of accepting what is, finding serenity in the present, and being guided towards inner peace and wisdom.

समर्पण की माधुरता में, ताक़त पाओ,
हर घड़ी, ज़िन्दगी में आनंद लाओ।

Sweet Surrender

In the realm of life's sweet surrender,
Find peace in letting go, remember.
No defeat in this release, it's true,
Path where blissipline shines through.

Stop the battle, cease the inner strife,
Let life's flow take its course, this life.
For there's wisdom in accepting the "no,"
In detached attachment, strengths grow.

The more you fight, drained you'll feel,
Let the storm pass, let the pain reveal.
Greys may linger, but they too shall fade,
Welcome the colours that life has laid.

Life's a journey, with twists and turns,
Don't let your fatigue's fire burn.
Surrender brings forth latent might,
Embrace the rest, ready for the light.

In surrender's grace, find your inner power,
Harnessing potential in each passing hour.
Be ready for the nectar so sweet,
Life's mysteries, in surrender, meet.

Oh, surrender, and wise just be,
Accept in life what's meant to be.
Let go of should-haves, embrace the now,
Guided to a place where serenity shall bow.

MYSTIC FLOWERS: GARDEN OF LIFE

(Pic by the author of Hillside Wild Flowers)

Being born into a Fauji family and then transforming into a Tankman, I have traversed the length and breadth of the country. Incredible India is a world-in-one nation with its diverse geography, rich heritage and incredible flora and fauna. Be it an assignment or a holiday, what captivated me most were the mystic wildflowers in the higher reaches of the mountains and plateaus. Certainly, the 'Valley of Flowers' in Sikkim was most breathtaking and a heaven on earth. It captivated my inner being and made me equate life to heaven on earth – *'Jannat'*.

'Mystic Flower's: Garden of Life', is a poetic journey through the tapestry of existence, where wildflowers symbolise the free-spirited and imperfect souls that grace our paths. These resilient and vibrant blooms stand as a testament to the beauty found in imperfection, growing and glowing alongside life's journey. As they sway in the breeze and display their vibrant hues, they become steadfast companions in life's unpredictable journey. The poem explores the enduring connection between the human spirit and the wild beauty of nature and the impact of these on the garden of life.

कुदरत का तोहफा है फूल,
धरती को जन्नत बनाते फूल।
सदा मुस्कुराते रहना यूं ही,
जीवन का पाठ पढ़ाते रहना यूं ही।

Mystic Flowers: Garden of Life

In gardens of life, stories are sown,
I seek mystic flowers, beauty known.
Imperfect souls, in nature's embrace,
Beauty and strength, a timeless grace.

Scattered souls, untamed and bright,
Dancing with winds, in soft sunlight.
They grow and flow, a vibrant stream,
Painting my path with nature's dream.

Amidst wild meadows, they proudly stand,
Bowing to no rules, no master's command.
Vibrant hues, gentle and wild display,
Lighting my journey in, my special way.

Each passing breeze, their ballet's thrill,
In their steadfastness, I find my skill.
Growing, glowing, wild and free,
Mystic wildflowers are love's decree.

In their imperfections, I see my own,
In their presence, my heart is known.
They're my companions, hand in hand,
In this romance, memories afresh stand.

In love's eternal garden, let them unfurl,
Blossoms of passion, a dance in this world.
My heart and soul, they deeply perceive,
Among wild flowers, life's mystic weave.

LIFE'S SPLENDOUR:
A SYMPHONY OF HEARTS

(Pic by the author taken on a Bali Cruise)

COVID-19 was a time of unprecedented turbulence and a timeless learning of many life lessons. It served as a great leveler and brought about the best in me. From a re-attired soldier to a COVID Warrior, it was a blessed journey of joy and contentment as a *'Human for Humanity'*. The joy was not the numerous accolades or awards I received, but the humbling messages from those whose lives I could save or make a difference in their world. I believe these were God's blessings.

We should take inspiration from the sun and work constantly for the benefit of mankind so that peace and prosperity prevail everywhere. - Sama Veda

'Life's Splendour: A Symphony of Hearts', explores the intricate tapestry of human existence. It delves into the profound dichotomy between the life often lived, marked by selfish desires, and the life aspired to, rich with love, kindness, and purpose. The poem beckons readers to awaken their inner light, to radiate love and grace, and to confront life's challenges with unwavering optimism. The poem serves to realise humanity's potential for greatness, encouraging us to become beacons of light and seekers of positive change in a world yearning for compassion, caring, and sharing.

ज़िंदगी की रंगीन रफ़्तार में,
हर पल एक कहानी, हर लम्हा प्यारा,
इंसानियत और हमदर्दी जब साथ है यहाँ,
ज़िंदगी के मंज़र में, लग जाए सितारा।

Life's Splendour: A Symphony of Hearts

In life's embrace, a gift divine, we trod,
A comedy of choices, guided by each nod.
In every moment, a chance to craft our story,
With love, and dreams of boundless glory.

Life's canvas painted with desires, emotions,
Seeking truth, bliss, in profound devotions.
A cyclic pendulum of time's enduring rhyme,
A journey of consciousness through endless time.

Selfish love, passion, and fleeting lust,
Transform into respect, care, and trust.
Canvas of humanity waiting for colours to ignite,
Humans for Humanity to pave the endless flight.

Life's song awaits, rhythm ever strong,
A story told since the world was young.
A garden needing care, roses to be tended,
Truth unfolds, its mysteries never-ending.

In the symphony of life, our souls entwine,
Like the selfless radiant sun and moonshine.
Moment's fleeting, gratitude forever to stay,
As we navigate life's path, come what may.

Awaken friends, spread love, grace's embrace,
Embrace challenges, wear a smiling face.
Kindness, a beacon in sorrow's dark hour,
Generosity's light, a force to empower.

WHISPERS OF SILENCE

(Image Courtesy: www.fotocommunity.com/ George Digalakis)

I am not a very talkative person, and on the lighter side, especially after marriage. Yet speaking, oration, and debates have been part of my persona since my school days. As one grew in service and rank, and matured, the responsibility of presentations and discussions cum talks on matters professional became more demanding and intense. Post-retirement, they flourished through seminars, webinars, podcasts, online interviews, and TEDx talks. Yet, being a man of few words, I enjoyed my moments of solitude and whispers of silence, both through meditation and more often being lost in a world of my own. They seem to do the magic of rejuvenation on me. Silence is a source of great strength. They say *'silence speaks when words can't'*.

'Whispers of Silence', is a poetic encapsulation of my moments of solitude that delves into the transformative power of silence, memory, and intuition. In the serenade of silence, the verses reveal a path to healing, self-discovery, and resilience. It evokes a sense of peaceful retreat, the serenity of solace and the discovery of the path to self-actualisation.

ख़ामोशी की भी अपनी ज़ुबान होती है जनाब,
ऐसे ही दर्द-ए-दिल से कुछ बातें कर लेती हैं लाजवाब।

Whispers of Silence

In the whispers of silence, I find my retreat,
Drowning in solitude, moments soft and sweet.
Inhale the memories, both gentle and kind,
Exhale the regrets, let them drift, unwind.

Within the soul, intuition a guiding light,
Moments of insight, as wisdom takes flight.
Unwavering, a blazing spirit does emerge,
To shine and conquer, from within, it'll surge.

My inner sanctuary, a realm of gratitude,
Whispers of silence, so tender and shrewd.
Choices I make, lead this journey of time,
Woven with positivity, in life's grand design.

In the depths of my soul, a fire gently glows,
Igniting my passions, like the morning's rose.
In the quietest moments, I chart my way,
As the serenade of silence continues to sway.

In the calm of solitude, I discover my grace,
Embracing each challenge, I'll find my place.
With each sacred breath, this journey I embrace,
Strength and grace within me, I forever chase.

So let the whispers of silence forever be near,
Guiding you through life, calming your fear.
Embrace the reality of endless possibilities,
In the whispers of silence, find your serenity.

AWAKENING OF LIFE'S ESSENCE

(Image Courtesy: soundcloud.com)

My journey of awareness through Vedanta and Atmabodha gave light to many a philosophical question that had remained unanswered in life. I was far from rituals of chanting daily prayers, yet God fearing with my inner silent prayers. Spirituality for a soldier was a distant horizon which only emerged closer post-retirement. It answered many questions and yet raised even more to oneself. It continues to be a blissful and never-ending divine journey. *'The essence of life lies not in the pursuit of happiness but in the noble quest to be useful, honourable, and compassionate, leaving a lasting mark through a life well-lived.'*

I close this book with this philosophical poem to resonate a chord in your blissful life. May you find the joy of awakening in yourselves.

'Awakening of Life's Essence', is a poetic expression of the divine questions surrounding human existence and the purpose of life. The poem touches upon the endless pursuit of finding the identity of self and the ultimate goal of achieving Moksha, a state of infinite bliss.

"तत्त्वमसि" *(Tat Tvam Asi)*

This Mahavakya is from the Chandogya Upanishad (6.8.7). It means **"Thou art That."** *It signifies the identity of the* **individual self (Atman)** *with the* **ultimate reality (Brahman)**, *emphasising the oneness of all existence, which aligns with themes of self-realization and the quest for purpose.*

Awakening of Life's Essence

Looking at the mirror, I asked, "Who am I?
"What is the purpose of my life?" I sighed.
An inner voice replied, "Transcend ego's cry,
Infinite love and compassion, let them soar on high."

Beyond worldly gains, our purpose takes flight,
The Universe craves love's tender light.
Erase 'I' and 'My,' in eternal knowledge's embrace,
Awakened minds, true selves divinely interlace.

Self-realisation, the wise soul's noble quest,
Reveals the truth, where the heart finds rest.
Moksha, life's grand and ultimate scheme,
Infinite bliss, the supreme dream.

Survival's mere prelude, in life, we shall strive,
Love and enlightenment, the path we derive.
Suffering, the offspring of ignorance's bane,
Shatter the chains, and end the ego's reign.

Flawless knowledge, wisdom's radiant guide,
Mistake-free, the ego's grip untied.
No penance, no strife, in this life we revive,
Break ignorance's chains, let your soul come alive.

Beyond mere survival, life's purpose we nurture,
Thriving, in love, our essence we uncover.
Embrace the Self, let your soul take its flight,
In enlightenment's embrace, find the divine light.

EPILOGUE

This book represents my heartbeats, embarking on a poetic journey into the sacred realms of the unknown. It navigates the intricate paths between the body, mind, and soul of a Tankman and a Soldier4Life. Through its pages, it forges a trail through the mystics of spirituality, valour, love, humour, and humanity.

I hope it has bestowed upon readers the enchantment of a soulful odyssey brimming with smiles, emotions, and profound introspection into the gift of being blessed humans for the betterment of humanity.

As a soldier, the valour and sacrifices of our 'Fallen Bravehearts', and the well-being of their brave families stand paramount, echoing a sentiment that should resonate with every citizen who enjoys safety and wellbeing courtesy of them.

With heartfelt gratitude, I bring the curtains down on this literary venture, extending my best wishes to all.

God Bless and Godspeed.

यत्र योगेश्वर: कृष्णो यत्र पार्थो धनुर्धर: |
तत्र श्रीविजयो भूतिध्रुवा नीतिर्मतिर्मम || **(BG 18.78)**

(Wherever there is God Almighty, the master of all mystics, there will also certainly be opulence, victory, extraordinary power, and morality.)

www.ingramcontent.com/pod-product-compliance
Lightning Source LLC
LaVergne TN
LVHW061611070526
838199LV00078B/7247